FAITHBOOK

First Edition Published in 2023

Ahlulbayt Islamic Mission (AIM)
aimislam.com

ISBN: 978-0-9957589-4-0

© AIM Foundation 2023

All rights reserved. No part of this publication may be reproduced, stored in a retrieval system, or transmitted in any form or by any means, digital, electronic, mechanical, photocopying, recording, or otherwise, or conveyed via the internet or a website without prior written permission of the publisher, except in the case of brief quotations embodied in critical articles and reviews.

IN THE NAME OF GOD, THE MERCIFUL,
THE COMPASSIONATE

Contents

Perface 1

Chatper 1: Formulating Your Worldview 5
Worldview: An All-Inclusive Perspective on Life 6

Chatper 2: The First Cause 11
Faith and Science 12
The Intelligent Designer 13
Proof of God's Existence 15
Belief in God through Intuition 32
The Attributes of the Divine Designer 41

Chatper 3: The Purpose of Creation 55
Existential Concerns 56
Deriving Meaning from Life 57
Purpose of Existence 63
Purpose of Human Existence 67

Chatper 4: The Human Need for Religion 83
What is Religion? 83
The Miracle of the Quran 98

Chatper 5: Man as Vicegerent 107
Trials and Tribulations 110
Servitude 118
Divine Mercy 121
Human Vicegerency 123

Perface

> *And Allah brought you forth from the wombs of your mothers knowing nothing, and He gave you hearing and sight and hearts that you may give thanks.*
>
> –Quran 16:78

> *"If one were to tell an unborn child that outside the womb there is a glorious world with green fields and lush gardens high mountains and vast seas, with a sky lit by the sun and the moon, the unborn would not believe such an absurdity. Still in the dark womb how could he imagine the indescribable majesty of this world? In the same way, when the mystics speak of worlds beyond scent and color, the common man deafened by greed and blinded by self-interest cannot grasp their reality."* [1]
>
> -Rumi

---

1. Mafi, Maryam; Melita Kolin, Azima. Rumi's Little Book of Life: The Garden of the Soul, the Heart, and the Spirit. Hampton Roads: 2012, p.7.

WAVES OF physical agony herald the arrival of a human being into the world. The unrelenting tides of pain rise and collapse until the awaited moment finally and blissfully arrives. The overwhelmed newborn wails at the world, expressing his first surge of human sentiment; then with barely open eyes in a tiny crumpled face he is soothed and swaddled snugly into the crook of his mother's arm.

The depth of his experience remains obscure to the adults who eagerly crowd around him to take a first glimpse of his features. Struck by a sudden feeling of astonishment at being thrust into an unfamiliar world, the newborn innately grasps that he is a part of a wider existence which contains a kaleidoscope of faces, forms and colors. Nestled comfortably in his mother's womb, he had been oblivious to the wider world encircling him, but his post-birth shock awakened him to a hitherto hidden reality. And now ensconced in his mother's embrace, close to the heartbeat which had comforted him for nine months, he finds solace and shelter from the wide, awe-inducing world.

These initial moments of wonder usher a lifetime of exploration. In rapid succession, the newborn develops mentally and emotionally with the aid of social interaction and sensual perception. He becomes familiar with his immediate surroundings and forges bonds with his family members, gradually attaining knowledge of his environment. He dotes on his mother and fears the dark, but possesses no general concept of motherhood nor does he understand the reason behind the absence of light. With time, he develops memory and imagination, communication skills and conceptual knowledge.

The human pursuit for knowledge begins at a very young age. Not only do young children explore their physical surroundings, but they also display curiosity toward the grandest intangible reality: God. They wonder about God's external appearance and his actions, asking their parents questions about Him: *Where is he? What does he look like? Can I see Him? Can He give me everything I want?*

With the passage of years and the advancement of cognitive development, humans acquire in-depth knowledge of concepts and theories, their contemplative capacities expanding and their viewpoints broadening in scope. The simple, basic questions which they once asked metamorphose into existential questions: *How did I come into existence? Why do I exist? What is the purpose of life and death? Where am I heading?* These inquiries take on a momentous character: "The answers to these questions should have the highest priority in life because if we get them wrong, we will get everything wrong. If we do not find answers for them, we will find nothing at the end. Even if we gain the entire planet with all its wealth, fame and pleasure, we are doomed to lose it all. Thus, everything will become ultimately meaningless".[1]

These profound questions represent a human attempt to understand the meaning of existence and the fate one will inevitably meet. They form a common quest for truth which unites humans regardless of their race, language, geographical region and time period. Archeological expeditions have revealed drawings, inscriptions and statues which clearly exhibit the existential concerns of ancient populations. When one contemplates the pyramids of Egypt, the picturesque Roman ruins scattered all over the Mediterranean, or the ancient constructions of Mesopotamia, one swiftly realizes that these existential concerns occupied human beings in ancient times as well.

Scientific advancement and technological development have not obliterated these points of concern in our modern day. With the emergence of new scientific theories, secular modernists falsely claimed that science would uproot existential concerns, but reality has proven them wrong. No discoveries or scientific achievements have remotely succeeded in eliminating this sense of wonder from the inherent human consciousness[2].

---

1. Aydin, Necati. Said Nursi and Science in Islam: Character Building through Nursi's Mana-i Harfi. Routledge: 2019.

2. Einstein himself strove to discover satisfying answers to existential questions and eventually reached the conclusion that his deep reflection on existential truths was an innate and spiritual function. In a letter to his friend, the Queen Mother Elisabeth of

This book takes you on a journey to delve into your innermost thoughts and embark upon a personal experience of faith. It highlights the framework of an Islamic worldview and presents the fundamental concepts of intelligence design, the purpose of creation and the need for religion. It encourages you to seek answers to your existential questions and to earnestly follow revelation, translating your beliefs into fruitful action. It awakens you to your eternal fate, inspiring you to search ardently for the meaning of life and urging you to forge a connection with the source of your existence, the soother of your soul, and the healer of your heart: Allah.

Belgium, Einstein wrote: "The strange thing about growing old is that the intimate identification with the here and now is slowly lost. One feels transposed into infinity, more or less alone."

Isaacson, Walter. Einstein: His Life and Universe. Pocket Books: 2008.

Chapter One
Formulating Your Worldview

> *"Muslim religious doctrine promotes a concept of the entire material universe as a sign of God's activity, a creation by God, which God upholds. Thus, in order to understand God, it is necessary to investigate every aspect of his creation."*[1]
>
> -*Howard R. Turner*

LET'S ASSUME you are an undergraduate student at medical school and are currently studying human physiology and anatomy. You are discovering the fundamental concepts of cellular biology and learning how cells are structured, how they divide to produce tissues, and how they function. You are also exploring the organization and regulation of the human genome. With trillions of cells in your body performing precise and multiple activities every second of your life, you can't help but marvel at the complexity of the human body.

Or let's suppose you prefer physics –the science that studies matter, motion and energy in the universe. You enjoy learning about quantum mechanics and celestial phenomena, and are currently studying the law of motion set forth by Isaac Newton or the modern theory of gravitation formulated by Albert Einstein. Electricity, magnetism or thermodynamics is your favorite field of knowledge.

The examples go on. Whether you are studying biological sciences such as biochemistry and medicine, or the physical sciences which include the fields of astronomy and chemistry, the more knowledge you acquire the further will you realize that the information which falls beyond the range of your knowledge far exceeds what you know. A thought-provoking quote is attributed to Socrates: "The more I learn, the more I

1.Turner, Howard R. Science in Medieval Islam. University of Texas Press: 2010.

realize how much I do not know". It is a wisdom paradox. At the start of your education, you will feel elated at acquiring large amounts of knowledge, but with time and the discovery of more information you will realize that there are still so many things to learn. Uncharted land forever lies ahead of you.

Knowledge of the material world consists of scientific data but remains narrow in scope. The laws, principles and observable phenomena of scientific disciplines provide a reply to your question: *"How?"*, but fail to present an answer to your unrelenting question: *"Why?"* You know that cells form the basic building blocks of your body and that they combine to form tissues and organs that perform vital functions, but why do these organs exist in the first place? You are aware that physical laws govern the universe, but who placed them? Did an intelligent power create the cosmic system we live in?

Existential questions inevitably arise in the minds of human beings at one point or another. The various fields of natural sciences provide an explanation for observable phenomena, but only the mind aided by the light of wisdom may reach answers to grand questions which are represented by the three-syllable word: *"Why?"* From here, it is pertinent to understand the meaning and significance of the worldview which forms the cognitive foundation of an individual.

WORLDVIEW: AN ALL-INCLUSIVE PERSPECTIVE ON LIFE

A worldview is your broad outlook to life and the universe, and consists of the fundamental beliefs you hold. It represents your comprehensive interpretation of existence. Humans investigate the world from two aspects; from one point they examine the details of animate and inanimate objects -their shapes, sizes, and colors- and from the other they inquire about their roles in the intricate system which they are a part of.

Suppose you are formulating theories regarding the sun. From one vantage point, you view the sun as an enormous star which lies at the heart of our solar system and converts hydrogen to helium for the generation of light and heat. But from another much deeper perspective, you realize that the sun is a part of this fine-tuned universe and a key requirement for life on earth, created by an intelligent power. This second explanation becomes part of your worldview. You no longer view the sun as merely one star among billions of stars scattered in space, but a creation essential for existence and therefore the fulfillment of the divine plan for humanity.

Similarly, you might consider something much smaller in size and less consequential like a squirrel scampering from one tree to another. You might study its diet, breeding habits and defense mechanisms, but from another aspect you might examine the significant ecological role this small rodent plays in ensuring the sustainability of its habitat and in improving forest regeneration. Through this second comprehensive examination, you realize that squirrels have been created to play an active role and ensure ecological equilibrium.

There are various synonyms for the term "worldview": intellectual perspective, outlook to life, and overall viewpoint, to name a few. This special term has become universal in our modern times: "The term *worldview* is derived from the German word *Weltanschauung*- a concept originally coined by Immanuel Kant (1790) in his work *Critique of Judgement*… Kant introduced the concept of *Weltanschauung*, composed of *Welt* (world) and *Anschauung* (view or outlook), to describe the human ability to create order in a complex world that is full of infinite possibilities for perception. For Kant, a worldview was hence a comprehensive vision that enables human beings to see and experience and come to term with the world."[1]

A worldview is reached through contemplation and analysis. Through cognition, you form your own worldview and base your actions upon it. Suppose you are sitting with guests in your living room. You "see" them and are communicating with them, but you are simultaneously calculating the remaining

---

1. Juergensmeyer, Mark; Sassen, Saskia; Steger, Manfred B. The Oxford Handbook of Global Studies. Oxford University Press: 2019, p.159.

time for the kettle you placed on the kitchen-stove to boil. In your mind, you "see" the kettle on the stove and have mentally calculated the time the water needs to reach its boiling point. If one of your friends wanders into the kitchen after the time is up and returns to tell you that the water hasn't boiled yet, you immediately realize that something is wrong. This example clarifies how a person may reach certainty through cognitive processes, even though something as simple as boiling water doesn't have an effect on an individual's life. A person's worldview, however, is critical because it makes life meaningful and acts as a "doctrinal force that forms people's psychological, spiritual and intellectual lives, moving them to principled action." [1]

Let's consider another example. Suppose you are driving your car in the countryside on a brilliant summer day, and your friend is sitting next to you. You pass through a grove of citrus trees that has not borne fruit yet, and you try to recognize the nature of the trees: will they bear tangerines or oranges? From the color and size of the leaves you speculate that they are tangerine trees, but your friend thinks otherwise. Each of you tries to draw on your botanical information to support your opinion, and you engage in a short discussion on citrus trees. This dialogue has no effect on your trip; you are merely passing the time until you reach your destination where you will soon forget your exchange. But suppose you have lost your way. Your debate acquires a different nature and things become more complicated when you have opposing opinions. Your friend insists that you took a wrong turn, but you believe you are on the right track. Your argument has now gained significance because it concerns your destination; you have to slow down and ask for directions or check a navigation application to pinpoint your location. You both know that if you continue on a wrong route, you will only get farther away from where you are heading.

---

[1] Abu Sulayman, Abdul-Hamid. The Qur'anic Worldview: A Springboard for Cultural Reform. International Institute of Islamic Thought: 2013, p.3..

From this example, we may glean insight into the importance of one's worldview. What is the point of traversing a familiar life itinerary -receiving primary education, graduating from university, finding work, getting married, establishing a family, and finally retiring- when all of these phases are not driven by a deeper meaning? How can a person mentally and psychologically cope without providing answers to existential questions? Would you enroll at an institute of higher education without first exploring the curriculum and setting personal goals for your education? Would you accept an unpaid job which absorbs your energy and hides your talent? Every person performs his/her daily actions with a set of objectives in mind, so how could you possibly live your life without a purpose? In line with this clarification, a worldview is an overall perspective which influences all aspects of your life: the food you choose to eat, your work, your method of worship, your moral principles, and the rules of social conduct you abide by.

A worldview of a person who believes in God radically differs from that of a person who rejects his divine origin. This difference is not merely restricted to oral expression of one's beliefs and perspectives, but is clearly reflected in the general manner of living. A believer has a beacon of light to guide him when he is lost, a shelter during life's storms, and a spring of water in the desert of desolation, while a person who has no faith wanders aimlessly, hopelessly, tantalized by mirages and illusions.

Belief in a Creator impacts your thoughts, emotions and behavior. It imbues life with a purpose that can never be attained in the shadow of a materialist worldview that attributes existence to blind chance. There is a vast difference between living life wholesomely with a sense of meaning, knowing that a wise Creator brought you forth into existence and has a plan for your life, and between illogically believing that your existence is a result of a random process.

A religious worldview provides fortitude in times of crisis, offers solace during hardship, and revives hope even when there seems to be no imminent relief on the horizon. Belief in God is the essence, the light which brightens your life, the source of your strength. It molds your identity and shapes your destiny. This is why it is pertinent to proceed from the first and foremost principle, the belief in God, to understand your place in the world.

Seek God with a sincere heart, and see how He will bring you to Him, gently and lovingly.

Chapter Two
The First Cause

❝

*"Open the window of your heart
And look at the Beloved's Face.
Love's task is to create that window
So His beauty may illuminate the heart.
It is in your power, my friend,
To gaze constantly at the Beloved's Face."*[1]
-Rumi

W E ARE BORN BELIEVERS. Humans have an innate disposition toward religion and the belief in a Higher Power. A three-year international research project, directed by two academics at the University of Oxford, found that humans have a natural tendency to believe in God and the afterlife. The £1.9 million project involved 57 researchers who conducted over 40 separate studies in 20 countries representing a diverse range of cultures. The studies, both analytical and empirical, concluded that humans are predisposed to believe in God and the afterlife.[2]

Human faith in God is diverse. Across various geographical regions, different populations have adopted a wide variety of religious worldviews, resulting in numerous ideas, perspectives and experiences. Religion has always played an active role in human life, but a new trend has emerged in the contemporary era. An anthropocentric view has been introduced which argues that human beings are the most significant entities in the world. This is a basic belief embedded in many Western philosophies where man views himself as the center of the world.

We now notice how the interest of human beings in many societies revolves around themselves, their desires, their personal capacities and capabilities. Man has become blinded

---

1. Rumi's Little Book of Life, p.79.
2. Ross, Tim. "Belief in God is Part of Human Nature -Oxford Study". The Telegraph. 12 May, 2011.

with preoccupation with himself, overlooking his divine origin and striving toward personal fulfillment. Faith has been pushed away from individual and social life, and science has been presented as an answer to life's questions.

FAITH AND SCIENCE

Contrary to what many adversaries of religion may claim, science actually *enforces* faith rather than destroying it. Islam has never proposed theories which contradict human experience or scientific findings; it urges humans towards progress and creativity and expects them to further the common good of humanity. It simultaneously imposes ethical regulations that prevent humans from exploiting their scientific achievements for personal interests, engagement in warfare, or monopolization of resources.

If you conduct a study of Muslim history, you will discover the positive outlook toward science and the propagation of learning in Islamic societies. Muslims have long enjoyed a rich legacy of scientific pursuit, encouraged and emphasized by their religion: "Commanded by the Quran to seek knowledge and read nature for signs of the Creator, and inspired by a treasure trove of ancient Greek learning, Muslims created a society that in the Middle Ages was the scientific center of the world. The Arabic language was synonymous with learning and science for 500 hundred years, a golden age that can count among its credits the precursors to modern universities, algebra, the names of the stars and even the notion of science as an empirical inquiry."[1]

This lies in stark contrast to the historical persecution of scientists by church authorities during the Middle Ages in Europe. For instance, the Italian astronomer Galileo was put on trial in 1633 for publishing evidence supporting the Copernican theory which states that the earth revolves around

---

1. Overbye, Dennis. "How Islam Won, and Lost, the Lead in Science". The New York Times. Oct.30, 2001.

the sun. He was found guilty of heresy and spent the rest of his life under house arrest.

In Islam, however, there was never a contradiction between science and religion whether in theory or in practical application. Islam allows science to present explanations for natural phenomena but never neglects the ultimate Cause behind them. For Muslims, these phenomena demonstrate the magnificence of God and the immensity of His power. Muslims are urged to contemplate the world around them to observe God's signs. In Muslim belief, "such an effort to comprehend is essential in attaining the just and righteous life that forms the earthly part of a person's purpose as proclaimed by the Prophet. A simpler, more expressive spiritual motivation for scientific inquiry, let alone metaphysical investigation, is difficult to imagine."[1]

THE INTELLIGENT DESIGNER

Imagine yourself standing outside on a clear dark night gazing at a sky studded with hundreds of blinking stars. Have you ever asked yourself how this enigmatic beauty came to be? The scientific community agrees that the universe had a beginning billions of years ago. Accounts of the origin of the universe explain how the universe expanded from an initial state of high density and high temperature. After this expansion, the universe cooled sufficiently to allow the formation of particles that later coalesced to form stars and galaxies.

Scientists have examined the cosmos meticulously yet one question still confuses them: *What existed before the universe came into being? If the universe had a beginning, what is the nature of the previous entity or system? If it is of a material nature, then what existed before it* (taking into account that scientists unanimously agree that material substances occur at a certain point in time).

---

1. Ibid.

Some bizarrely allege that the universe was created from nothing despite the logical improbability of this happening. It is common-sense to inquire: Since *when did something spring from nothing?* "If any reader only partially comprehends the scientific facts concerning the Big Bang, the universe, and the fine-tuning necessary for its 13.7 billion years of existence, then the case is closed. There can be no other explanation, and modern science has proved it. Those supersized numbers, such as ten to the fortieth power, as calculated in fine-tuning, alone demand intelligent design."[1]

Suppose someone asks you: "Who taught you French?" If you name someone who doesn't understand a single word of French, the listener will stare at you incredulously, fully aware that it is logically impossible for someone who is ignorant of a certain language to teach it to others. Or assume that your brother confided in you that he had received an amount of money from a person you know is destitute. Wouldn't you immediately conclude that the poor man you once pitied is displaying a false façade of poverty? Then why are we expected to believe that the exquisitely fine-tuned universe was the product of a random process?

The universe holds many mysteries that continue to perplex astronomers in modern times, but what is known is that "a closed or isolated system such as the big bang, which obeys natural law, cannot of itself produce order out of the disorder of an explosive beginning. How many new buildings have resulted from simply setting off dynamite? Our universe certainly did not come about by the uncontrolled, wildly random forces of the big bang."[2]

Material philosophies have failed to provide answers to life's questions. Karl Marx, for example, discussed the philosophy of dialectical materialism and strove to reach a theory explaining the material elements in the universe, yet he gave no account

---

1. Rock, J. Howard, Universal You–And the Big Bang. 2012, p.113.
2. Hatch, Durwood B., God Did It: Not the Big Bang and Evolution. Tate Publishing and Enterprises: 2010, p.94.

of existence prior to the presence of physical phenomena, nor did his materialist philosophy succeed in providing healing answers to existential concerns. The proponents of atheism have never succeeded in presenting a single piece of evidence on the non-existence of a majestic intangible force. Defeated and frustrated, they try to hide their irrational allegations by propagating misleading statements or theories which they claim are "scientific", but which are in truth absurdities driven by psychological and social factors devoid of any logic. From here, we proceed to present two methods which produce evidence on the existence of the Supreme Being.

Proof of God's Existence

1. Rational Inference

Einstein was once asked during an interview: "Do you believe in God?". Clearly expressing his convictions, he answered: "I'm not an atheist. The problem involved is too vast for our limited minds. We are in the position of a little child entering a huge library filled with books in many languages. The child knows someone must have written those books. It does not know how. It does not understand the languages in which they are written. The child dimly suspects a mysterious order in the arrangement of the books but doesn't know what it is. That, it seems to me, is the attitude of even the most intelligent human being toward God. We see the universe marvelously arranged and obeying certain laws but only dimly understand these laws."[1]

Prominent intellectuals throughout history and across various cultures have formulated numerous logical arguments on the existence of God. Aristotle introduced the concept of the Prime Mover, and thinkers such as Rene Descartes, Baruch Spinoza, Avicenna, and Mullā Ṣadrā all presented evidence on the existence of God.

---

1. Einstein: His Life and Universe, p.386.

You can achieve belief in God through logic. When you head to work or your institute of education, you encounter various intricate networks on your way –electrical transmission, communication lines, and the transportation system to name a few. You understand beyond any doubt that all of these structures have been designed and constructed by specialists. On a larger scale, logic also dictates that the magnificent universe could not have come into existence by chance or by a stroke of luck.

Suppose you set out from your house early in the morning, leaving it in a state of disarray. Papers and pens are scattered on your desk, clothes are tossed on the floor, and your pillow is lying near your bed. But when you return home at night, you find your papers and books placed in convenient order, your clothes folded and tucked in your closet, and your bed neatly arranged. You immediately realize that someone has been into your home and tidied it up. You try to guess who it might be, but if none of your family members or friends have the keys to your house, you are overcome by apprehension at the thought of a stranger entering your home and moving your belongings around. All the same, it would not cross your mind for the slightest instant that your home was tidied on its own. Your common-sense dictates that there is no action without an actor and no design without a designer even if you weren't there to witness it happen.

The earnest concern with discovering your origin indicates how serious you are and reflects your willingness to live a meaningful life: *"To what or to whom do we owe our existence?* This has to be the starting point for people who take life seriously-scientists and non-scientists alike. We cannot rest without the answer, because absolutely everything of importance is riding on it. To know where everything came from is to know where we came from, and where we came from has everything to do with who we are, and who we are has everything to do with how we ought to *live.*"[1]

1.Axe, Douglas. Undeniable: How Biology Confirms Our Intuition That Life Is Designed. HarperCollins: 2016.

Rational inference not only proves the existence of an intelligent Designer of the universe, but it also asserts His wisdom and power. It is impossible for random coincidence to produce the complex life forms or to create the intricate cosmic system we live in. There *must* be a Supreme Power which created all the wonders of the universe for a purpose. This shall be elucidated through three prerequisites.

A. Design in the Universe

If the universe were not designed, laws and principles would lack relevance. Design lays the foundation for math, physics, chemistry, biology, astronomy and medicine. A law or principle has no function in a chaotic world. The universe functions in conformity with natural laws which intricately connect its various parts. Water boils at 100°C, condensation of water droplets in the atmosphere results in rainfall, and oxygen is produced by photosynthesis. But who placed all of these laws in the first place?

Any functioning system requires a founder and an overseer. Manufacturing factories operate according to certain laws and require electricity and energy. There must also be a capable administrator to manage a factory and sufficient manpower to ensure effective production. On a larger scale, we can observe multiple processes, mechanisms and functions in the universe. The presence of intricacy points to the Creator, the highly organized nature of the universe points to the Organizer, and the operation of laws indicates that there is a Placer of laws.

While you are reading these words, several cognitive and neuropsychological functions in your brain are at work. Your eyes perceive the visual information on the printed page and your neurological system is stimulated. If you lose a single capacity, your reading skills will be considerably weakened.

You are staring at these printed words at this moment, but have you ever stopped and considered the amazing faculty of vision? The eye consists of highly complex anatomical structures. Light enters the eye through the cornea which consists of thousands of neurons. Unlike almost every other part of the body, the cornea has no blood vessels and therefore no color. A clear cornea is essential for vision. Without the ability to maintain a blood-vessel-free cornea, our vision would be significantly impaired.

Then comes the retina which turns light into signals and images. The retina contains photoreceptor cells which are divided into rods and cones. There are over 100 million rods in the retina which function in night vision, and around 6 million cones which are responsible for color vision. Nerve impulses carry information about the image to the brain through the optic nerve. The optic nerve then carries the sensory nerve impulses from more than one million ganglion cells toward the visual centers in the brain. All of these tiny structures are at work while you are reading!

This intricate system requires an outer line of defense. Eyelashes protect the eyes from small particles such as dust, sand or debris, and also help filter out the sunlight that shines onto your eyes. Blinking cleans the ocular surface of debris and flushes fresh tears over it. This brings nutrients and other substances to the surface structures to keep them healthy, helps prevent infection, and brightens the image which is received. There are two types of gel-like fluids inside the eye which help it maintain its shape, and this plays an important role in overall eye health. Close your eyes and imagine what life would be like without vision. The elaborate components of the eyes and the highly delicate structures involved for vision point to the loving Creator who allowed you to see.

If you move on to another aspect and contemplate the atmosphere of the earth, you will discover that the high oxygen content of earth's atmosphere is "out of the ordinary". Oxygen is a highly reactive gas that is supplied continuously by biological processes; without life. The sun provides necessary light and heat but also emits ultraviolet rays. Go outside on a fine day and feel the warmth of the sun on your face. What happens when a cloud passes over? You'll notice that the cloud takes away some of the heat and light coming from the sun. In much the same way that a cloud blocks the heat on a hot day, the ozone layer in the stratosphere blocks out the sun's deadly ultraviolet rays. Even a 1 percent reduction in the amount of ozone in the upper atmosphere can cause a measurable increase in the ultraviolet radiation that reaches the earth's surface. If there were no ozone at all, the amount of ultraviolet radiation reaching us would be catastrophically high. All living things would suffer radiation burns, unless they were underground, wearing protective suits, or in the sea[1]. How could this calculated precision be a result of chance!

Using "*If*" in conditional sentences serves to emphasize the wondrous aspects of the universe. "Those who work in fundamental physics encounter a world whose large-scale structure (as described by cosmology) and small-scale process (as described by quantum theory) are alike characterized by a wonderful order that is expressible in concise and elegant mathematical terms"[2].

We can state some assumptions to assert the intended meaning. We know that the earth is perfectly shaped and positioned in space to allow life, but what would happen if changes occurred to the bright blue planet which we call home? The following conditional sentences will give you a glimpse into some wonder-inducing facts.

If the earth were smaller, its atmosphere would lose oxygen and water vapor, causing temperature levels to rise to a degree inhospitable to life.

If the earth were twice as big, its surface gravity would double. It would become more difficult for us to walk, and plants and trees would topple over.

---

1. Professor Neville Fletcher, Australian Academy of Science.
2. Polkinghorne, John. Belief in God in an Age of Science. Yale University Press: 1998, p.2.

If the earth were closer to the sun, our climate would become significantly hotter. Warming would cause glaciers to melt, raising sea levels and flooding most of the planet.

If the earth were farther away from the sun, our planet would freeze and oceans would become covered in ice.

If the earth had no tilt -with the axis of its rotation remaining perpendicular to the plane of orbit- we would have no seasons and the surface temperature on earth would be the same during winter and summer.

If it weren't for the composition of Earth's atmosphere -21% oxygen and 78% nitrogen which regulates the surface temperature- then temperatures would have widely varied between night and day.

If the oxygen content in earth's atmosphere increased, combustion would occur more energetically and life would be adversely affected. With the presence of more oxygen, forest fires would become more devastating, and everything would burn more easily.

If oxygen were less abundant in the atmosphere, respiration would become difficult. We would also have a decreased amount of ozone gas (O3) in the upper atmosphere which shields the earth's surface from deadly ultraviolet rays.

Similar assumptions can be made regarding the human body.

If humans had no endocrine glands which are responsible for hormone production, then growth, metabolism, mood, and reproduction capacities would not function properly.

If humans had no exocrine glands which excrete enzymes, problems would arise in the regulation of body temperature and the secretion of sweat and saliva. Mothers would also not be able to breastfeed their babies.

If humans had no white blood cells which flow through the bloodstream to fight viruses, bacteria and other foreign invaders, they would fall prey to illnesses.

If humans had no friendly bacteria lining their digestive tracts, the growth of harmful bacteria would not be controlled, production of vitamin B_{12} and vitamin K would be inhibited, and certain substances such as fiber would not be digested.

This is just a short list! There are thousands of other examples which demonstrate the fine-tuning of the universe and the precision in the human body. All of these examples point to the Creator, leaving no vestige of doubt. Countless proof may be presented which corroborates that the marvelous order in the universe is the handiwork of God.

"We will show them Our signs in the horizons and within themselves until it becomes clear to them that it is the truth. Is it not sufficient as regards your Lord that He is a Witness over all things?"

(Quran 41:53)

B. Design Requires a Designer

Innumerable examples in the fields of physics, chemistry, astronomy and mathematics prove beyond any doubt that the complexity in the largest celestial objects to the smallest of particles is an indicator of intelligent design. To prove intelligence design, we may proceed from a principle instinctively realized by all people regardless of their education level: the universal law of causality.

The law of cause and effect is dominant in all fields of scientific knowledge. Legend has it that a young Isaac Newton was sitting in his mother's garden deep in contemplation when an apple fell on his head. This led him to examine why apples fall vertically to the ground and not horizontally, and eventually inspired the theory of gravitational force. Newton not only realized that the earth exerts a gravitational pull, but he also discovered that bodies in the universe attract one another in proportion to their respective masses. An apple exerts a gravitational force, but due to the earth's larger mass, the gravity of the latter is greater and this leads to the attraction of the apple toward earth. Newton eventually published his book *The Mathematical Principles of Natural* Philosophy in 1687 in which he introduced the universal force of gravity.

All innovations and discoveries contributing to scientific advancement are a result of extensive research into causality. Take the ebb and flow of the sea for example. Scientists have studied why the water level of the ocean rises and then subsides during the day, leading to the conclusion that both solar and lunar gravitational forces cause the movement of tidal waves.

There are numerous examples which verify that the universe is a vast network that adheres to the law of causality. Through the principle of cause and effect, scientists have provided answers to phenomena such as global warming, changes in air pressure, pollution, and the extinction of flora and fauna. Causality not only applies to scientific principles. Researchers in humanities closely examine the causes of social phenomena such as poverty, unemployment, racism, divorce, and crime, in addition to psychological traits such as confidence or introversion. Reliance on causality is a standard procedure which all humans follow, regardless if they are religious or not. If a small machine requires a designer, how could the huge and mind-boggling universe have no Cause?

C. Precision in Design

The signs of manifest precision in design point to an intelligent Designer. When you observe ancient works of construction such as the pyramids of Egypt, or modern structures such as skyscrapers, robotic machines or satellites, you will notice the precision in construction and admire the skill of the builder.

Humans instinctively realize that an action requires a performer, and that intricacy in the end-product indicates the performer's ingenuity. Suppose you are observing a painting and taking several factors into account: its aesthetic qualities, visual representation, and artistic pattern.

You notice that the color composition is superb and that the artist has used a fine technique to portray the subject matter. Your positive impressions lead you to admire the artist's talent and the masterful transformation of the canvas into a mode of expression. This sensation is also evoked when you listen to a musical symphony, or when you read fine poetry. Innovators, constructors, and artists are awarded in ceremonies in honor of their achievements and in recognition of their ingenuity and high skills. All of these human innovations in art, engineering, and communication technology emanate from the brain's astonishing capacity.

Our universe provides an intricate image; a sky studded with constellations of stars and dotted with planets moving in their orbits, a blue planet conducive to life, formed of geological layers and enveloped by an atmosphere retained by earth's gravity, and a great diversity of living organisms on earth. Upon considering these phenomena, the only logical probability is that the elaborateness in life's manifestations arises from an intelligent and powerful Designer.

Coincidence from a Social Perspective

Suppose you usually take a certain path when cycling to work, but one day decided to follow another road for sightseeing. On the way, you meet an old childhood friend whom you have been striving to find on social media for a long time. It seems likely that your first exclamation after calling out his/her name will be: "What a coincidence!"

Or suppose that since you graduated from university you have spent months searching for a job but with no result. One day, you enter a grocery store and hear a customer complaining on the phone that he still hasn't found an employee. You focus on what he is saying and discover that he needs someone specialized in your field of knowledge. You muster the courage to approach him after he hangs up and inquire where you should apply for the job. A few days later, you're hired! When you recount these incidents to your family members and friends, they will immediately express their surprise. You repeat the word "coincidence", but you are fully aware that the striking occurrence of two or more events at one time is extremely remote.

These two examples are relatively simple occurrences, but matters become even stranger if they are applied at the cosmic scale with the presence of highly intricate and interconnected parts. How could the complex order of the universe be a result of mere coincidence?

Suppose a crime occurs where a notable businessman is murdered while exiting his company and the money he had been carrying is not found. No one will believe that the victim was killed coincidentally by a stray bullet, that he happened to be carrying a large sum of money, or that someone passing incidentally by found the money lying near the victim's corpse and decided to steal it and flee before the arrival of anyone on the scene. All of these interconnected incidents can't be a result of coincidence. If the thief is found and he claims that he happened to be present at the scene and that he had not plotted to steal the victim's money, investigators will immediately dismiss his account.

Coincidence is often attributed to unexplained phenomena or causes. "The overstuffed crate labeled 'coincidences' is packed with an amazing variety of experiences, and yet something more than rarity compels us to group them together. They have a similar texture, a feeling that the fabric of life has rippled. The question is where this feeling comes from, why we notice certain ways the threads of our lives collide, and ignore others."[1]

When two things are moving toward one another while you are unaware of the trajectory of one of them, you might attribute their convergence to coincidence. Let's assume you woke up to beautiful weather and decided to go hiking, unaware that a lunar eclipse was expected that day. When you reach the summit of a hill, you sit down to enjoy the sprawling

---

1. Beck, Julie. "Coincidences and the Meaning of Life". The Atlantic. February 23, 2016

view but you suddenly notice a subtle change in the atmosphere and realize that a lunar eclipse is occurring. You murmur to yourself: "What a coincidence!" But suppose you had checked your calendar beforehand and knew that a lunar eclipse was expected that day but decided to go hiking anyway, you would not have been surprised in that case.

Sometimes incidents occur according to a plan developed in advance, but when you are unaware of this prior adjustment you might attribute it to coincidence. Considering events from an incomplete and individualistic perspective might lead a person to attribute events to chance, while a holistic contemplation of the universal order and the trajectory of causes leading to the meeting of two entities will result in an explanation.[1] This not only applies to everyday life but to the intricately designed cosmos as well. The meticulous design and arrangement of the universe leaves no doubt as to its creation by an Intelligent Cause with awe-inspiring attributes, and this may be demonstrated scientifically

Coincidence from a Scientific Perspective

Probability theory is a branch of mathematics which studies the probability or improbability of the occurrence of an event, taking into account several factors. Mathematics posits a value of probability which is either null or 1. If the result of the mathematical equation is null, the occurrence of a certain event is impossible, and if the result is 1 the probability of occurrence is certain. Probability theory predicts certain or impossible events and divides the value of possibility over the value of other possibilities.

The final result falls between null and 1.

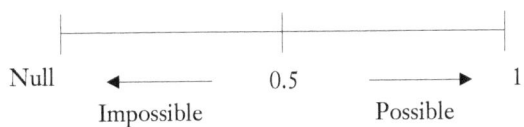

---

2. Motahari, Mortada. Al-Tawhid. Dar al-Hawraa, 2003.

For instance, if warm clouds are moving toward a given point while another group of cold clouds is floating toward the same point with a speed that renders the collision of both cloud formations inevitable, the probability of rainfall will be 1. This is attributed to several factors that determine precipitation such as the type of clouds and the speed and direction of the wind. But if warm clouds are moving in a certain direction at a speed which does not allow collision with cold clouds, the probability of rainfall will be close to null. This calculation is a process adopted by weather stations to forecast the weather.

Take another example into consideration. Suppose that a bowl containing 7 balls, four white and three red, is placed in front of you. You close your eyes and reach for a ball. The possibility of extracting a white ball is the number of white balls (4) divided by the total sum of balls in the bowl (7) which equals to 0.6. At the same time, the possibility of extracting a red ball is the number of red balls (3) divided by the total sum of balls in the bowl (7) and this equals 0.4. Therefore, the probability of extracting a white ball is greater than the probability of extracting a red ball.

Let's take this example a step forward. If a bowl contains 49 red balls but only one white ball, the probability of extracting a red ball is 49/50 which equals 0.98, a sum which is close to 1. On the other hand, the probability of extracting a white ball is 1/50 which equals 0.02, an almost impossible probability. The more the probabilities increase in number, the possibility of obtaining a specific result decreases until it becomes mathematically impossible. For instance, the probability of extracting a single white ball in a bowl which contains 999 red balls is the extremely remote sum of 0,001.

Let's consider another example. The English alphabet consists of 26 letters. Suppose you shuffle small cardboard cutouts of these letters in a bowl and randomly choose four letters, placing them in order of extraction. What is the probability of choosing four letters that spell: HOPE? This word consists of four letters, and to reach the probability of extracting each letter, 1 is divided by the total number of letters in the alphabet (26). Therefore, the probability of extracting these letters in order is: $\frac{1}{26} \times \frac{1}{26} \times \frac{1}{26} \times \frac{1}{26} = 0.00000218829$ a sum which is almost equal to 0.

These mathematical results are not surprising. Suppose a strange man enters a room where you are sitting with nine friends and you playfully ask him to guess your names. He points at one of you and immediately guesses his name. You are all surprised but you leave room for chance, assuming it was just a lucky guess. But if he points to the second person and guesses his name correctly, you will start to wonder. If he goes on to guess the names of the third and then the fourth person, none of you would believe it was just a stroke of luck. You will automatically assume that someone had previously informed him of your names because you know that successive accurate guesses are impossible without prior knowledge.

The meticulous order in the universe, the interconnection between its parts, and the inhabitability of earth are all indications of purposeful design. The complexity in the mechanisms of the universe points to the glory of the Designer. The theory of probability gives weight to intelligent design over any other explanation. Belief in design entails the existence of an intelligent designer while materialism demands irrational belief in random chance despite the fact that the probability of undirected processes producing complex results coincidentally is zero.[1] Mounting evidence on organization in the universe eliminates the probability of coincidence and establishes belief in the wisdom and power of the Creator.

Proteins, the basic building blocks of living cells, are made up of amino acids that join together to form long chains. The sequence of a protein is determined by the DNA of the gene that encodes the protein. A change in the gene's DNA sequence may lead to a change in the amino acid sequence of the protein. Changing just one amino acid in a protein's sequence can affect the protein's overall structure and function. The Swiss physicist Charles-Eugène Guye examined these factors and through

---

1. Al- Sadr, Muhammad Baqer. Mujaz Usul al-Din. Dar al-Hadi: 2000, p.154.

his calculations concluded the impossibility of a coincidental combination of protein sequences. The probability of the coincidental formation of one particle is, $\frac{1}{10^{160}}$ an estimate which is equal to zero.[1]

Scientific Laws and Coincidence

Scientists avoid presenting explanations by resorting to coincidence and adopt a logical rule stated by the philosopher William of Ockham (1285–1347/49). "Occam's razor" is the principle that, of two explanations that account for all facts, the simpler one is more likely to be correct. It is applied to a wide range of disciplines, including physics, astronomy, mathematics and medicine. This principle entails favoring the least complicated evidence when the results of several pieces of evidence are equal to one another. Isaac Newton expressed his adherence to this principle, stating: "We are to admit no more causes of natural things than such as are both true and sufficient to explain their appearances"[2]

According to the British physicist and astrobiologist Paul Davies, "In science, one tries to avoid appealing to flukes. Occam's razor entreats us to try the simple and obvious explanations first. But sometimes simple and obvious explanations just won't work, and we are forced to invoke something out of the ordinary. As Sherlock Holmes remarked, when you have eliminated the impossible, then what remains must be the truth"[3]. Davies excludes "the odds against a sequence of lucky accidents extending unbroken over billions of years, generation after generation. No human lottery would dare to offer such adverse odds."[4] Therefore, the only remaining logical explanation is that an Intelligent Cause created this world and all that is in it.

---

1. Belief in God in an Age of Science, p.15-16.
2. Varela, Charles R. Science for Humanism: The Recovery of Human Agency. Routledge: 2019, p.282.
3. Davies, Paul. The Goldilocks Enigma: Why is the Universe Just Right for Life. Mariner Books: 2008, p.136.
4. Ibid.

Davies explains: "Among the many prerequisites for life –at least, for life as we know it- is a good supply of the various chemical elements needed to make biomass. Carbon is the key life-giving element, but oxygen, hydrogen, nitrogen, sulfur, and phosphorus are crucial too. Liquid water is another essential ingredient. Life also requires an energy source and a stable environment, which in our case is provided by the sun. For life to evolve past the level of simple microbes, this life-encouraging setting has to remain benign for a very long time; it took billions of years for life on Earth to reach the point of intelligence. On a larger scale, the universe must be sufficiently old and cool to permit complex chemistry. It has to be orderly enough to allow the untrammeled formation of galaxies and stars. There have to be the right sorts of forces acting between particles of matter to make stable atoms, complex molecules, planets, and stars. If almost any of the basic features of the universe, from the properties of atoms to the distribution of galaxies, were different, life would very probably be impossible."[1]

According to Fred Hoyle, the British astronomer who famously coined the term "Bing Bang", the fine-tuning of the universe indicates that life began in space under the direction of a great intelligence.[2] "Once we see, however, that the probability of life originating at random is so utterly miniscule as to make it absurd, it becomes sensible to think that the favorable properties of physics, on which life depends, are in every respect deliberate...It is, therefore almost inevitable that our own measure of intelligence must reflect higher intelligences...even to the limit of God."

Therefore, it is logically inevitable to conclude that the precision in the universe is a result of divine intelligence. This leads us to submit to the fact that the universe has been wisely and meaningfully designed in a manner conducive to human life.

Suppose a seed falls in the soil next to a punctured pipeline, receiving a steady supply of water. The seed has the potential

---

1. Ibid., p.2.
2. Hoyle, Fred. Evolution from Space. Roya Institution: 1982, p.12

to grow into a plant or even a fruit-bearing tree when the circumstances are favorable, but this has nothing to do with chance. Nature is not a wise force which causes transformations in living organisms. Transformation arises due to the inherent potential God places in species to grow and change in suitable circumstances. Take in vitro fertilization for example, the process where an ovule is combined with a sperm in a laboratory context to facilitate the conception of a child. The process is rendered successful because the sperm and ovule have the potential to fuse together and develop into a human being when the circumstances are favorable.

Proponents of evolution are faced with the following question: Where did species gain the capacity for improved transformation? They are at a loss to provide a credible answer because there must be a Supreme Power which *guides* natural processes. Furthermore, evolution fails to explain abstract matters such as human consciousness, intelligence, innovation and freewill. Therefore, when we witness the brilliant and complex canvas of creation, we turn toward the Power whose attributes of omnipotence, wisdom, and innovation are reflected in the world of existence.

2.Philosophical Argumentation

Philosophical evidence does not rely on sense perceptions, and this explains why empirical disciplines fail to refute philosophy. Some individuals find philosophical contemplation somewhat difficult, especially in our modern times which are marked by an increased reliance on the senses at the expense of deep reasoning. The following examples are an attempt to make the concept easier to grasp.

When you are walking outside, you encounter a multitude of people and a variety of objects. The common factor between all of them is *existence*, an obvious concept which needs no clarification. All things that you see were once *non-existent*, and they came into being at one point in time. Take a large celestial object like Mars for example, or a tiny microscopic virus like covid-19; they both currently exist but at one point they were non-existent and then came into being. You also know that in the future, new things might come into existence like your potential grandchildren or a cure for a disease. Everything that had a beginning and came into existence, or that may potentially exist in the future, is called a finite being, and every *finite being* needs a *cause*.

The human mind can reflect upon an entity which has existed since eternity and needs no cause to come into being because existence is *inherent* to it. When you say that something began to exist, it means that it came into being at a certain point in time. However, a being above time who was never in a state of non-existence needs no cause to come into existence and is called an *Infinite Being*. Existence is an essential quality of the eternally existent Being who bestows life on all the living organisms we see. This concept might seem difficult to grasp, but it may be clarified by a scientific example.

According to Einstein's theory of relativity, time is linked to space and there can never be one without the other. "You can't have time without space, or space without time, so if space cannot be continued back through the big bang singularity, then neither can time. This conclusion carries a momentous implication. If the universe was bounded by a past singularity, then the big bang was not just the origin of space, but *the origin of time* too. To repeat: *time itself began with the big bang.*"[1] Therefore, existence prior to the Big Bang was *beyond* time and space. This may aid in clarifying the concept of the Infinite Being who is beyond the dimensions of time and space. When there is no past or future, there is no point in speaking of a cause for the Infinite Being who is *beyond* time.

Infinite Regress or "Tasalsul"

Islamic theology provides evidence on the uncaused Infinite Being through various argumentations, among them the impossibility of infinite regress. The word *tasalsul* (regress) is derived from the word *silsila* (sequence, series, range), with the root meaning of chain. In philosophical parlance, the term

---

1. The Goldilocks Enigma: Why is the Universe Just Right for Life, p.69.

means infinite regress, or endless chain. This argument states that life could not have arisen from an endless chain of causes without a beginning. Take the following example for instance: You are a finite being with a cause x, while the cause for x is y, and the cause for y is z and so forth. In the end, there must be a first uncaused cause –the Infinite Being- or you would be trapped in a never-ending chain of causes. Hence, *tasalsul* is impossible because it implies a continuous chain of dependent causes that have no beginning point.

If dependent causes extended to infinity, nothing would have existed in the first place. For instance, if an instructor asks volunteer (a) to plant a tree, but (a) says he won't do it unless (b) plants a tree, while (b) insists on planting a tree only after (c) does, then no tree would be planted at all. Or if a poor person asks a passerby for money and he promises to pay only if a second passerby pays, while the second passerby promises to pay if a third one does and so on, then the poor man would receive no money. This is why *tasalsul*, the dependence of a thing's existence on the fulfillment of an infinite number of conditions, is impossible.

Finite beings are dependent beings that require a cause for existence. Finite beings can be causes for one another (like parents and their children), but all dependent beings need a final uncaused cause, the Independent and Infinite Being, the cause for all living entities we see. If you contemplate existence, you will realize that all finite beings rely for their existence on God, *"the Light of the Heavens and Earth"*(Quran 24:35).

Belief in God through Intuition

Humans may reach direct perception of truth through intuition as well. Aided by this inner perception, one may reach belief in God. The mind can logically infer the presence of an imperceptible and nonmaterial force that created the universe, a belief which is reached through conscious mental processes but is also embedded in humans since childhood

According to *The Guardian*, "developmental psychologists have provided evidence that children are naturally tuned to believe in God of one sort or another. Children tend to see natural objects as designed or purposeful in ways that go beyond what their parents teach... Rivers exist so that we can go fishing in them, and birds are here to look pretty. Children doubt that impersonal processes can create order or purpose. Studies with children show that they expect that someone -not something- is behind natural order."[1]

This instinct to believe is not only restricted to children. Researchers at Harvard's Psychology Department conducted a study linking religious belief to intuition and found that "there is something in the cognitive makeup of humans that promotes belief in a higher power. For example, the natural tendency that people have to see a purpose behind random events, or the need to reduce uncertainty in their lives -as well as the anxiety it causes- may promote a belief in God."[2]

You don't need anyone to explain your innermost feelings to you such as sorrow, fear or hate. When you love someone -a parent, spouse, or child- you feel a warm personal attachment toward that person. You are aware of your emotions without necessarily possessing a detailed knowledge of the concept of love or its reasons.

It is important to always keep in mind that humans have a spiritual and material aspect, even though many branches of knowledge in our modern times neglect the spiritual dimension. Humans have basic organs such as eyes, lungs and blood vessels, but they starkly differ from animals due to their possession of cognitive capacities such as linguistic expression, moral discernment, abstract thought, creativity and freewill. These distinctive traits explain the human domination of the world and how humans have developed from living a primitive life to inventing remarkable technologies; from living in tents erected amidst sand dunes in the desert and fire-lit

---

1. Barrett, Justin, "Out of the Mouth of Babes", The Guardian. 25 November 2008.
2. Powell, Alvin. "Intuitive? Try God". The Harvard Gazette. September 20, 2011.

caves snuggled within lone mountains to building skyscrapers which soar above the clouds and jets that fly faster than the speed of sound.

Not only do humans possess intellectual abilities, they also have intuitive capacities which are implanted in them. "We can do a lot of things intuitively: we can intuitively produce and interpret utterances, we can intuitively estimate the distance of an approaching vehicle, we can intuitively predict the trajectory of a thrown baseball. These are intuitive capacities in the sense that we can exercise them without reasoning or conscious reflection: they are spontaneous, effortless, and 'automatic'."[1]

Belief in God is intuitive: "Knowledge of God's existence is self-evident. It requires no education, reflection or evidence. It is contained in the innate nature of man *(fitra)*, which is universal and unchanging."[2] We can refer to two types of inner perceptions in humans:

A) Axioms

Axioms are self-evident truths which require no proof. Underlying the processes of science are "axioms" or "first principles" which are necessary for making inferences from scientific data. Every field of knowledge requires fixed preambles to obtain answers to unknown issues. For example, "the whole is larger than the part", "nothing can be existent and non-existent at the same time", and "parallel lines never meet" are all axioms which the mind grasps without the need for proof. There are also axioms of morality and ethics such as "all humans must be treated with justice" and "oppression is condemnable".[3]

---

1. Biggs, Stephen; Geirsson, Heimir. The Routledge Handbook of Linguistic Reference. Routledge: 2021, p.556

2. Leaman, Oliver (editor). The Qur'an: An Encyclopedia. Routledge: 2006: p.351

3. René Descartes, the French mathematician and philosopher, decided to take an original course of action to reach knowledge. He decided to doubt everything, even self-evident truths, dismissed apparent knowledge derived from the senses, and erected new foundations on the basis of the intuition that when he is thinking, he exists. He found that he could not doubt that he himself existed -as he was the one doing the doubting in the first place- and he expressed this in the famous dictum "I think; therefore, I am". He

As previously mentioned, we instinctively know that every finite thing has a cause. If you find a professionally sculpted sandcastle on the seashore, would you possibly believe that the incessant lapping of the waves resulted in its construction? The attention to detail which is evident in the sandcastle's construction indicates the expertise of the builder, and this may never be attributed to the sea.

Our intuition states that this vast universe has a cause. The axiom of causality is applied to everything we witness in the world. If the simplest phenomenon requires a cause, how could it be claimed that this awe-inducing universe existed without one? This instinctive knowledge is inherent in all people, from nomads to philosophers. Where does this urge arise from? It emanates from an inherent inclination toward the sacred, a religious instinct which is present in highly educated individuals and primitive tribes alike. There is a force within you which pulls you toward God and constantly calls you to Him.

B) Instinctive Knowledge

Instincts are inborn patterns of activities or tendencies, typically performed in response to specific external stimuli. All humans possess natural inclinations which are not taught or acquired by experience. For instance, new-born babies display an instinctive sucking reflex which enables them to consume milk. Once humans grow up, they display other inclinations and tendencies such as self-preservation.

The pursuit of knowledge is also a human inclination. Aristotle begins his treatise called *The Metaphysics* by saying: "All men by nature desire to know". Children as young as three years old ask their parents dozens of questions to appease their curiosity and their innate love for exploration. Adults retain this inquisitiveness and eagerness for knowledge. It is recounted that the renown Muslim polymath Abu Rayhan al-Biruni was on his deathbed when a jurist came to visit him. As soon as the

---

was aware that without a firm basis, he could not proceed in knowledge formation. From this philosophical principle, he progressed to prove a set of issues, most importantly the existence of God.

jurist entered, al-Biruni asked him a question related to Islamic jurisprudence. When al-Biruni sensed his visitor's surprise, he remarked: "To die knowing the answer is better than dying while I am ignorant of it."[1]

Another significant natural inclination in humans is the love of perfection which is displayed in the pursuit of perfections –whether real or perceived- such as higher learning, financial stability, fame, physical fitness or outer beauty. Humans seek to remove their flaws or shortcomings and amass the largest number of perfections. It is remarkable that as soon as an individual achieves one perfection, s/he automatically seeks a higher one and is not satisfied with what he/she has attained.

This natural disposition is expressed by the psychotherapist Alfred Adler when he states that: "Mankind has variously made the attempt to imagine this final goal of human development. The best conception gained so far of this ideal elevation of mankind is the concept of God. There is no question but that the concept of God actually includes this movement toward perfection in the form of a goal…"[2]

Humans are inherently attracted toward perfection, and God is the possessor of the ultimate perfection. Even if you are not aware of it, you are inclined toward the unlimited power and wisdom possessed by God. Just as thirst and hunger are indications of the body's need for water and food, the religious instinct universally found in humans is an indicator of the need to form a connection with the Creator who possesses all the attributes of perfection. When humans sense a deficiency in themselves, they instinctively turn to the source of all perfection.

This inclination is further emphasized when an individual is in urgent need of the aid or intervention of God. When you suffer a setback, you instinctively resort to a superior power

---

1. Motahari, Mortada. Bayn al-Minbar wal Nahda al-*Husayniya*. Dar al-Irshad: 2009, p.40.
2. Edited by Carlson, Jon; Maniacci, Michael P. *Alfred Adler Revisited*. Routledge: 2012.

that will alleviate your distress. Fear, weakness, or poverty aren't the reason why religion was "invented" as some state; they rather *reveal* the inherent religious instinct in humans which drives them toward God.

This inner inclination toward God becomes manifest in times of peril. In the case of violent turbulence on board a flight, an imminent natural disaster, or danger lurking nearby, the fear which besets humans is coupled with an urgent devotion to a supreme power. The religious instinct is awakened and a person finds his solace in supplication, invoking God for protection.

If belief in God is intuitive and instinctive, why do some people drift away from God?

There are certain circumstances, however, which may affect recourse to God in certain people. Overall well-being and satisfactory conditions of existence may lead some individuals to be unmindful of God, but when misfortune befalls them, the first sentence which they instinctively utter is "Oh my God!" As Will Durant remarks: "The old belief that religion is universal is substantially correct. To the philosopher this is one of the outstanding facts of history and psychology…What are the sources of the indestructible piety of mankind?"[1]

The genuineness of the religious inclination is manifest through the following two realities. First, this instinct is common to all humans, regardless of their ethnicity, geographical region, or academic level –from the indigenous people living in the Amazon rainforest and the hunter-gatherer tribes in Africa to the halls of Harvard and the Sorbonne. "The moral and religious instinct, the instinct of the Divine is primordial in man, anterior and superior to every religion and every philosophy, the aliment and the foundation of every religious belief and of every philosophical speculation. This

---

1. Durant, Will. Our Oriental Heritage: The Story of Civilization. Simon and Schuster. Volume I.

alone is common to all men, savage or civilized, ancient or modern…This alone constitutes the unity of mankind."[1]

Technological advancement, scientific innovations and cosmic discoveries have not eliminated this innate religious instinct from humans. Even non-believing scientists admit to a great power behind the existence of the universe, while believing scientists consider that scientific findings strengthen their belief.

Albert Einstein, for instance, made his belief known: "Everyone who is seriously involved in the pursuit of science becomes convinced that a spirit is manifest in the laws of the Universe –a spirit vastly superior to that of man, and one in the face of which we with our modest powers must feel humble. In this way the pursuit of science leads to a religious feeling of a special sort, which is indeed quite different from the religiosity of someone more naïve."[2] Einstein also wrote: "My religiosity consists of a humble admiration of the infinitely superior spirit that reveals itself in the little that we comprehend about the knowable world. That deeply emotional conviction of the presence of a superior reasoning power, which is revealed in the incomprehensible universe, forms my idea of God."[3]

Second, this religious instinct is firmly rooted in humans; it functions continuously and can never be uprooted even though adversaries of religion strive to attack or dismiss it. Proponents of social theories such as Auguste Comte spoke of the "end of religious faith" and proposed science as a substitute for belief. The Communist Party in the Soviet Union destroyed mosques, churches and temples, executed religious leaders, and flooded schools and media with anti-religion propaganda. Furthermore, it introduced a system called "scientific atheism"[4]. Authorities strove over a period of seventy years to raise generations who

---

1. Saisset, Émile Edmond. Essay on Religious Philosophy. Turnbull & Spears. Volume 2, p.237.
2. Einstein: His Life and Universe, p.388.
3. Ibid.
4. Froese, Paul. "Forced Secularization in Soviet Russia: Why an Atheistic Monopoly Failed". Journal for the Scientific Study of Religion. Vol.43, No.1 (Mar., 2004).

shunned religion, but their attempts were an utter failure. "A belief in God remained a steadfast conviction for the majority of individuals throughout Soviet Russia, and the number of convinced atheists virtually disappeared after the fall of communism."[1] Religious devotion reemerged and thousands of orthodox churches were built or restored all over Russia. Today, Russian Presidents receive the blessings of the Moscow Patriarchate.

Andrei Bitov, a Russian novelist, grew up under the atheistic Communist regime, but one day his heart opened to the reality of God. He recalls, "'In my twenty-seventh year, while riding the metro in Leningrad (now St. Petersburg) I was overcome with a despair so great that life seemed to stop at once, preempting the future entirely, let alone any meaning. Suddenly, all by itself, a phrase appeared: Without God life makes no sense. Repeating it in astonishment, I rode the phrase up like a moving staircase, got out of the metro and walked into God's light.'"[2]

But if the religious instinct is common to all humans, why do we find irreligious people? This may be clarified through various points:

a) Some instincts and natural inclinations may become dulled due to certain circumstances. Take the maternal instinct for example. The surge of affection and protectiveness a mother feels toward her child is innate, and this instinct serves in establishing a special bond between the mother and her child. There are exceptions however and instances of mothers abusing their children emotionally, neglecting them, or even putting them up for adoption. This may be a result of the mother's own traumatic childhood, economic situation, or psychological problems. Just as certain conditions might affect basic instincts such as the maternal instinct, some circumstances have an effect on the religious instinct.

---

1. Ibid.
2. David Friend, ed., The Meaning of Life (Boston: Little, Brown, 1991), p.194.

b) Certain governments, educational facilities, and media outlets conspire to impose an attitude of irreligion and swerve youth away from faith. In schools and centers of higher education which adopt an anti-religion policy, certain subjects are exploited to further this aim, aided by modern technological tools. I have personally witnessed many of these instances at universities, and noticed how seeds of doubt were planted by a professor of natural science or a branch of humanities. If the student possesses no ample knowledge, s/he would inevitably be influenced negatively.

c) Some youth receive inaccurate religious information from their parents or friends, or even from clergy members who lack proper preaching skills. Teenagers might ask doctrinal questions sparked by curiosity, but instead of receiving satisfying answers, they might be met by simplistic and illogical replies or even by severe rebukes from traditional members of their family who believe questions regarding God and religion are a reason for condemnation. Young generations struggle to come to terms with the supposed opposition between religion and scientific findings, or to find explanations to what is falsely presented as genuine religious knowledge. If they don't achieve a correct explanation, they might start to think that religion is illogical and unnecessary.

d) Preoccupation with worldly affairs and the fulfillment of desires might cause humans to pay less attention to religion or to drift away from it. Religion holds humans accountable for their conduct and forbids unethical actions, leading some people to express dissatisfaction with "restrictive" teachings. Younger generations in particular experience a period of high energy and might suppose that happiness lies in breaking norms and testing limits. This revolutionary spirit and occupation with fulfilling cravings and urgings might lead to an estrangement from religion, but reality has shown that when adolescents grow older and rationality starts to dominate their actions rather than spontaneity and bodily cravings, many experience a return to religion.

The Attributes of the Divine Designer

The aforementioned scientific and philosophical evidence demonstrates the existence of God –the Designer, the Maker, the Organizer- leaving no room for doubt. From here, we may proceed to discover His divine attributes. The complex design we witness in the universe not only points to the presence of the Designer, but the aspects of design such as complexity, precision and beauty reflect His attributes. "Seeing the world as a sign of the perfect qualities of God is valuable because it means that passing things disclose enduring meanings. A beautiful flower eventually withers away, but through its existence and decay, it signified that its beauty is from the unending source of beauty that created both it and the other flowers that replace it (Nursi)."[1]

Creation gives us a glimpse of the qualities of God; every marvelous aspect we witness is an indication of His ultimate perfection. "Everything in creation, -including nature, history, and human life- points to these qualities of God. The created beings, in their beauty and decay, in their apparent power and weakness, reveal these names, the eternal Creator's power, knowledge, compassion, and beauty."[2]

Every finite creature needs the Infinite Being to come forth into existence, and all commendable qualities it possesses are granted by the Creator. Therefore, every perfection is attributed to God –the endower of perfections- to the highest and most sublime degree. Every excellence in finite beings reveals only a miniscule fraction of the beautiful qualities of God. Consider the radiant rays of the sun for instance; the warmth and light they provide are only small indicators of the enormous solar energy of the sun.

Fitra is a word used in the Qur'an which refers to the original disposition to faith that God instilled in humans. "The Qur'an refers in general to Islam as din al-*fitra*, which indicates that

---

1. Kynes, Will (editor). The Oxford Handbook of Wisdom and the Bible. Oxford University Press: 2021, p.228.
2. Ibid., 228.

human beings are inclined by their inner nature to submit to the Will of God; that it is inherent in human nature to aspire to the supreme good, to perfection, to both outward and inner purification."[1] Through the *fitra*, one may directly and inherently discover the attributes of God.

During times of need, the *fitra* is reawakened and one turns toward God and gains a sense of His divine qualities. Human beings innately strive to overcome their vulnerability, ignorance, poverty, or any other need by turning to God who possesses the ultimate power, wisdom, and self-sufficiency

We may understand divine attributes through the cosmic system. Precision in the universe indicates encompassing knowledge, the magnitude of energy therein reveals invincible power, and the structural orderliness of the universe and interconnectivity between its parts point to the oneness of the Creator[2]. In what follows, we shall consider some divine attributes more comprehensively.

1. Divine Knowledge and Omnipotence

"And with Him are the keys of the unseen; none knows them except Him. And He knows what is on the land and in the sea, and not a leaf falls but He knows it, and no grain is there within the darknesses of the earth and no moist or dry [thing] but [it is written] in a clear record."

(Quran 6:59)

God possesses knowledge of even the smallest details in the universe, and His power extends over all aspects of existence with nothing escaping from His domination. The two divine attributes of knowledge and omnipotence may be deduced from the complex design and numerical precision found in the cosmic system. No one can create something without being fully knowledgeable of its various aspects. Every expert maker has knowledge of his handiwork, and the production of his object indicates his ability. Whether it is an intricately weaved

---

1. The Qur'an: An Encyclopedia, p.211

2. Mujaz Usul al-Din, p.179.

carpet or a high-tech mechanical device, the end product is an indication of the maker's ingenuity and his ability to produce such a work.

Who knows how to fix a damaged electrical appliance more competently than the professionals who initially designed it? And who is able to construct buildings better than the engineers in charge of the project? On a large scale, we may ask: Who possesses more knowledge of the secrets of existence than the Creator who brought the entire universe into being? When you gain an awareness of the fascinating aspects of the universe, you will conclude the infinite power of God who assembled and organized its parts with breathtaking precision and harmony. When your awareness enhances, so does your belief in the absolute knowledge and power of God.

2. Divine Wisdom

Divine actions proceed from wisdom. Even though God possesses absolute power, He never acts arbitrarily. All of God's actions in the universe have a purpose, even though you might not comprehend it right away. In every divine action there is an obvious or hidden benefit.

Wisdom is defined as "putting everything in its proper place". A wise person displays wisdom in planning, allotment and distribution. For instance, a gardener knows that different plants need different amounts of water, shade and fertilizer, and that it would be unwise to place them all in the same conditions.

A-Understanding Divine Wisdom

God ordains, guides, and bestows according to wisdom. There are many references to God's wisdom in the Holy Quran, and this calls upon us to contemplate this divine attribute. "God is described as All-Wise [hakim] more than one hundred times in the Qur'an; the All-Wise is regarded as one of the beautiful names of God. The Qur'an repeatedly invites its audience to reflect on the world to witness God's wisdom. Nature is one locus of manifestation of divine wisdom. The Qur'an attracts attention to intentionality and purposefulness in nature, such as the benefits in wind and rain or the purposeful growth of a baby in stages, and shows them as signs of divine wisdom and power." [1]

We may comprehend divine wisdom through contemplating the intricate design in creation, the function of the universe, and the complexity of life organisms. For instance, the interrelationship between living organisms and the environment they live in presents a comprehensive image of a universe where both animate and inanimate beings harmoniously exist together to fulfill their successive roles. Every being in nature exists for a purpose which not only serves an individual advantage but also contributes to the collective good. In light of these observations, scientists have been trying to discover the essence of the wholistic system of life.

We should reflect upon the various aspects of creation as manifestations of divine glory. "Muslim thinkers as well as scientists have talked about the details of natural structures as disclosing the Creator's wisdom (Iqbal 2007, 16-26). They noted the placement of wise and beneficial results in balanced and intricate ways within the living beings and the rest of the world as revealing comprehensive divine knowledge and wisdom. Moreover, Qur'anic references to wisdom in creation encouraged impressive Muslim developments in science during the classical and medieval periods (Landau 1958). Contemporary Muslim approaches continue to value studying nature to appreciate God's wisdom."[2]

The wonders we see are signs which point to the Creator. "No sacred scripture of which we have knowledge speaks more about the cosmos and the world of nature than does the Quran, where one finds extensive teachings about cosmogenesis, cosmic history, eschatological events marking the end of the cosmic order as it now exists, and the phenomena of nature as revealing Divine Wisdom. In fact, the Quran refers to

---

1. Ibid., p.229.
2. Ibid.

these phenomena as *āyāt* ("signs," or symbols), employing the same word that is used for the verses of the Sacred Book. The Quran also speaks of life and its origin and of the relation of all beings, animate as well as inanimate, from animals and plants, to mountains, seas, and stars, to God... many Muslim sages over the ages have referred to the cosmos itself as a revelation, in fact the primordial revelation."[1]

Imperceptible Wonders

Consider insects for instance, those tiny creatures you might consider a nuisance. What role could they possibly play? The May 2020 issue of *National Geographic* magazine includes an entry on vital roles of insects in our ecosystem, where it mentions the following. It turns out that every buzzing, crawling, and hovering insect is a cog in the ecological machine! Insects are in nearly every food chain. Many larger animals-birds, bats, amphibians, and fish-eat insects before they in turn are eaten by predators. The death of insects is suspected to be a leading cause of recent declines in bird populations. Without insects, species that are higher up the food chain would suffer population losses.

Second, waste-eating insects unlock nutrients for use by the ecosystem that would otherwise stagnate in dung, dead plants and carrion, impeding the flow of nutrients. Furthermore, by feeding on crop-threatening pests, predatory insects perform the role of pesticides without chemicals. This cuts pest-control costs and increases yields, saving agricultural industries billions of dollars every year-while reducing toxic pesticide residue on crops.

Third, nearly 90 percent of flowering plant species and 75 percent of crop plant species depend on pollination by animals-mostly insects. Overall, one out of every three bites of food humans eat relies on animal pollination in the production process. A bumblebee can visit (and help pollinate) 3,000

---

1. Nasr, Hossein (Editor). The Study Quran: A New Translation and Commentary. Harper-Collins: 2015, p.26 (Electronic Format).

flowers a day. Without insects, crops can't reproduce, and humans and animals lose key food sources.[1]

Or take the process of photosynthesis for example. Photosynthesis is a chemical reaction that takes place inside a plant to produce nutrients which are essential for the plant's survival. The benefit of photosynthesis doesn't stop here. Most life on Earth depends on photosynthesis. The process is carried out by green plants which capture energy from sunlight to produce oxygen (O_2) and chemical energy stored in glucose. Herbivores then obtain this energy by eating plants, and carnivores obtain it by eating herbivores.

During photosynthesis, plants take in carbon dioxide (CO_2) and water (H_2O) from the air and soil. Within the plant cell, the water is oxidized, meaning it loses electrons, while the carbon dioxide is reduced, meaning it gains electrons. This transforms the water into oxygen and the carbon dioxide into glucose. The plant then releases the oxygen back into the air, and stores energy within the glucose molecules. Various factors are involved in this process such as sunlight, water, wind, soil, bacteria and green plants; all combine to serve an important purpose.

It would be impossible to overemphasize the importance of photosynthesis in the maintenance of life on Earth. If photosynthesis ceased, there would soon be little food or other organic matter on Earth. Most organisms would disappear, and in time Earth's atmosphere would become nearly devoid of gaseous oxygen.

Let's move on to another example, this time in the human body. The thymus gland is a small organ located behind the breastbone. Scientists previously thought that this gland had no function in the human body. It is large in infants and grows to reach its maximum size during puberty, after which it starts to shrink in size. It was later discovered that the thymus is an essential organ because it excretes the hormone thymosin which

---

1. Canales, Manuel; Elder, Scott. National Geographic. April 23, 2020.

regulates immunity. Before birth and throughout childhood, the thymus is instrumental in the production and maturation of T-lymphocytes, a specific type of white blood cell that protects the body from certain threats, including viruses and infections.

T-cells are "trained" for two years in the thymus to recognize pathogens and are "educated" not to attack healthy cells. Once this training period is over, T-cells are tested with an "exam" to see if they will attack harmful cells and avoid healthy ones. If they fulfill their duty successfully, they "graduate" into functioning cells. T-cells have the daunting task of recognizing and fighting off all the diverse pathogens that we encounter throughout our lives, while avoiding attacking our own healthy tissue. Though the thymus begins to decay during puberty, its effect in "training" T-lymphocytes to fight infections and even cancer lasts for a lifetime.

These are only a few examples among thousands of examples. Every living organism and natural process serves a purpose. Nothing has been created haphazardly. How can we not believe in the wisdom of the Creator while we continuously witness purpose in life? The more we study the meticulousness and meaningfulness in life forms, our belief in the wisdom of God is enforced. Divine attributes reflect the highest degree of excellence. God is not burdened by shortcomings or deficiencies; He has complete sovereignty over the universe and always places things in their proper place". This is why the human *fitra*, coupled with rationality, leads a person who is inspired with awe at the magnificence of creation to declare: "*Subhan Allah!*"

B-Significations of Divine Wisdom

Why isn't the Earth filled with gold? The answer according to divine wisdom is that there is no advantage in filling the entire planet with this precious metal. Gold would not retain its value if it were present in abundance and readily available to all people. Furthermore, the scarcity of this substance is a test for humans who are attracted to its glimmer. Will they strive to amass precious jewelry and refrain from paying charity? Will gold blind them to the purpose of their existence?

Divine wisdom extends over all aspects of life and underlies whatever you see. Based on this belief, the mind dictates that wherever there is a *true* benefit or advantage, God brings it into fulfillment. Whether it is the oxygen you breathe, or a peculiar fish swimming in the ocean, or a colorful tropical plant -God created everything for a purpose. If we self-centeredly estimate the value of phenomena according to our own interests, we would view their importance only in light of the benefits we reap from them. The criterion of divine wisdom, however, does not serve such superficial interests

Take the following anecdote for instance from *Aesop's Fables*. A father had two daughters; one was married to a farmer and the second was married to a tile-maker. The father asked his first daughter one day if there was anything he could do for her, and she answered, "I wish it would rain so that all the plants will be watered." Briefly afterwards, the father asked his other daughter the same question, and she replied, "I wish for continuous sunshine to dry the tiles." The father could not decide between the two and could do neither. Rain would benefit his first daughter, while sunshine would be to the advantage of his second one.

Therefore, if aspects of existence served the personal desires and narrow interests of human beings, existence would be devoid of rationality and chaos would reign. From this brief introduction, we may proceed to consider two highly significant implications of divine wisdom.

Aspects of Divine Wisdom (1): Guidance

Crop production requires careful attention to the soil, environmental conditions, water supply and the nutritive needs of society. Once seeds are sown, agricultural producers strive to provide an adequate nutrient supply and sun exposure for crops to grow to their full potential and to ensure an abundant harvest. But suppose you pass through a neglected field of produce and notice that the soil is cracked and the plants are withered. You will wonder what happened to the owner which prevented him from completing his project. If someone living nearby tells you that the farmer had planted this field "for fun" and never intended to harvest the produce in the first place, you would be surprised. No rational person would exert an effort for nothing. If someone embarks upon a certain project but deliberately neglects it halfway through, s/he would be described as careless and unwise. This principle can be applied to clarify the divine purpose behind the creation of mankind.

God created humans so that they can attain perfection. If God had created humans but refrained from guiding them to perfection, leaving them lost and helpless and unaware of the purpose of their existence, it would contradict divine wisdom. We may understand this by considering God's attributes. He who possesses the utmost perfection acts accordingly, and all His actions are meaningful. God wants humans to reach their full potential and aids them in making this possible.

Humans are unable to independently discover the path to perfection. The secret to human superiority on earth lies in mental and cognitive faculties and not in physical prowess. Humans have managed to tame wild animals, climb heights, and accomplish astonishing feats not merely through their physical capacities, but more importantly through their perception. One blow from an aging lion would kill a human while harsh weather would freeze him to death, but mental capacities have enabled mankind to dominate the planet. Humans have accomplished outstanding achievements yet have not answered the question: *How can mankind reach perfection and true happiness?*

Some people estimate happiness according to financial stability, health, employment and social welfare but wholly neglect the profound factors of inner joy such as spiritual tranquility, the fulfillment of supreme objectives, and adherence to lofty values. This paves the way for the following question: What is this perfection which human beings have been created to attain? Is it material strength according to Nietzsche, or self-rectification according to Gandhi? Is it the satiation of desires to the farthest degree according to Jeremy Bentham and Stuart Mill? Or is it the attainment of grand mental capacities which facilitate reasoning according to Avicenna? Or the eschewal of the worldly life and the purification of the soul according to Ibn al-Arabi?

Humans have differed on the definition of perfection and the ways to achieve it, and this disparity in itself is an indication of their incapacity to independently fathom perfection and their constant need for guidance in order to achieve it.

Understanding the meaning of perfection and the methods to achieve it requires knowledge of human nature, capacities and inclinations. The focus here is on the spiritual aspect. This process takes into account a human's journey in this world and his passage toward the hereafter, and the benefit of the mind, body and soul. All of this cannot be determined by limited human perception.

Human intellect determines that God necessarily guides humans to perfection. Suppose a school principal intends to introduce a new and effective educational method to teach students algebra. He knows that the students need capable teachers to help them comprehend this branch of mathematics, and that they would be unable to solve algebraic equations on their own. If the principal fails in assigning efficient teachers and in implementing the new academic program, parents will view him as incapable of reaching his goal or lacking the suitable knowledge or skill to do so. This may be compared to human life. Humans innately seek perfection but don't know the way or the appropriate means to do so on their own. This is why the dispatch of wise and competent prophets and messengers is necessary, as God in His wisdom and power would not leave His servants without mentors and guides to the Straight Path.

Aspects of Divine Wisdom (2): Immortality

Suppose you are spending a sunny day at the beach and notice a boy building a sandcastle. You both know that the waves will wash this sandcastle away sooner or later, but the boy is enjoying this temporary form of amusement. Even though there are more beneficial ways he could spend his time -like reading a book or cleaning away trash which is littering the beach- this form of enjoyment is not met with disapproval.

But suppose a person purchases a piece of land and pays a fortune to construct a stately home and fill it with luxurious furniture. He hires a professional interior designer and pays meticulous attention to detail, choosing the best fabric, flooring and elaborate ornaments. Imagine that after building this house, he doesn't move into it nor does he sell to anyone but decides to demolish it. If you ask him why he destroyed a construction he had spent so much money on and he answers that it was for his personal amusement, you would doubt his sanity. A boy building a sandcastle which the waves will wash away can't be compared to a mature person spending so much time, money and effort on constructing a remarkable home before deciding to destroy it for mere entertainment

In view of this reality, an important question arises. If death means the end of us, what is the point in exerting so much effort in life? Is this world worth all the struggle? Life swiftly passes by, and each person will undoubtedly face death. No matter the amount of knowledge one acquires, the sum of wealth he amasses, or the social status he reaches, his days will come to a close. Does death mark the end? Humans have been endowed with the instinct of self-preservation which is the strong inclination to remain alive and avoid perilous situations. Why do humans possess this instinct despite the fact that everyone will die sooner or later? Take hunger or thirst for example; when you eat or drink you satisfy your body's basic needs, but what is the purpose behind the instinct of self-preservation?

No material philosophy can provide a satisfying answer. You can only find a credible explanation in religion which states that humans have been created in this world to acquire ethical values and perform righteous deeds, paving the way for their eternal abode. You should not chain your soul to the worldly life but should make use of your existence in this temporary world to seek perfection and reap the divine reward in the hereafter. From here, we understand that the instinct of self-preservation is embedded in humans for a reason, and that fulfillment of this instinct occurs in the afterlife. Being aware of the eternal, blissful life which awaits you and exerting an effort to prepare for your final abode imbues your life with purpose.

What is the meaning of life? Philosophers have pondered this question for centuries while psychologists and sociologists have conducted research to arrive at an explanation. Despite their different inferences, many of them have agreed that belief in the hereafter raises an individual's positivity levels and mitigates psychological stress. This belief fulfills an inherent human need and confers meaning on one's existence on earth. Even though you may not see the results of your virtuous actions in this life, you will find recompense in the hereafter and gain inner serenity regardless of the hardships you face. This provides an incentive for progress, continuous improvement and advancement toward spirituality. Your efforts, tears, pain, suffering and patience are not in vain.

3.Divine Providence

Divine Providence is the care and guidance of God over the creatures of Earth. Individuals who believe in divine providence sense the absolute power and wisdom of God during every moment of their lives. They know that God moves the largest celestial objects in the sky and shows mercy to the tiniest fetus in its mother's womb. He provides humans with all their needs, facilitates their affairs, and encompasses them with compassion. Try to compare your capacities and potentials with the blessings you have received, and you will realize that God has shown you great benevolence.

When we understand the infinitude of God, we realize that our existence as finite creatures wholly relies upon His grace. Existence is not an indispensable aspect of finite beings; you might exist or not exist. And because you exist, it means God *wanted* you to exist. Your presence on earth is a gift from God. Even after we come into being, we remain in constant need of our Creator because our existence is derived from Him. Finite beings are in need of the Infinite Being for their existence and the *endurance* of their existence.

Rab is an Arabic word which is translated into *Lord* and means "one who manages affairs". Divine lordship signifies that "creatures are reliant on God in all their affairs" . The slightest movement in the vast universe occurs only by His leave. God's influence encompasses the entire realm of existence and extends over nature and humankind. His glory radiates with every sunrise, cascading waterfall, and blooming rose.

"God is kind to His servants; He provides for whomsoever He will, and He is the Strong, the Mighty."
(Quran 42:19)

CHAPTER THREE
THE PURPOSE OF CREATION

> "Only ignorance keeps a bird encaged.
> The Masters have fled from their cage
> and have become guides, showing that
> the only way out of ignorance is faith." [1]
> -Rumi

A QUESTION ARISES after establishing belief in our divine origin: *What is the purpose of creation?* Human beings are distinguished from other creatures with a sense of curiosity and concern for the future. At one point or another, they will halt and ask themselves: *"Why do I exist? What does the future hold in store for me?"*

Some brush this question aside after brief reflection, while others may choose to ponder it deeply and derive an answer which has a profound impact on their lives. "Although most people put the question of why we are created aside after occasional brief reflection, it is extremely critical for human beings to know the answer. Without knowledge of the correct answer, human beings become indistinguishable from other animals around them. The animal necessities and desires of eating, drinking and procreating become the purpose of human existence by default, and human effort is then focused in this limited sphere. When material satisfaction develops into the most important goal in life, human existence becomes even more degraded than that of the lowest animals."[2]

---

1. Rumi's Little Book of Life, p.12.
2. Phillips, Bilal. The Purpose of Creation, Dar al-Fatah: 1995, p.5-6.

Existential Concerns

The concern which human beings display toward their future plays a positive role as it drives individuals toward progress and leaves them unsatisfied with what they have attained. If humans disregarded their future, they would remain content with their daily sustenance and wouldn't plan ahead. This concern takes two forms; it might either be limited to the acquirement of material gains or may broaden in scope to become an existential concern which takes into account the purpose of creation and the meaning of life and death. This concern involves inquiring after the meaning of life, the purpose of creation, and the soul's destination after death.

Ancient civilizations exhibited concern with the afterlife through various methods, even though the details of their beliefs differed. For instance, the ancient Egyptians buried funerary artefacts in the tombs of the dead to ensure a proper afterlife. Pyramids were also built for religious reasons; the pyramid's smooth, angled sides symbolized the rays of the sun and were designed to help the pharaoh's soul ascend to heaven. Ancient Egyptians believed that when pharaoh died, part of his spirit remained with his body. To properly care for his spirit, the corpse was mummified, and everything the king would need in the afterlife was buried with him, including gold vessels, food, furniture and other offerings.[1]

Belief in the afterlife was also present ancient China. The ancient Chinese believed that life carried on after death. Tombs were arranged with objects people would need in the afterlife such as weapons, ritual vessels and personal ornaments. The mausoleum of the first Qin emperor of China -which was found to contain a Terracotta Army consisting of thousands of clay warriors, horses and weaponry intended to protect the emperor in the afterlife- is a very impressive example of Chinese belief in immortality.

---

1. Egyptian Pyramids. History.com. September 30, 2019.

Human societies have always been marked by religious sentiment and an outlook to the afterlife. Plutarch, an ancient Greek philosopher, is recounted as saying: "If we traverse the world, it is possible to find cities without walls, without letters, without kings, without wealth, without coin, without schools and theaters; but a city without a temple, or that practiseth not worship, prayer, and the like, no one ever saw." [1]

Humans may never find true tranquility and ease their worry before discovering the meaning of life and the purpose of their existence. An individual who has reached intellectual maturity should actively seek answers to existential questions and embark upon an inner quest to achieve knowledge, which in turn comforts and soothes him.[2]

DERIVING MEANING FROM LIFE

Have you ever stopped and thought for a moment when performing a certain action: *What is the point in what I am doing? Is it worth all the effort? Isn't this a waste of time?* These questions

---

1. Sweeting, George. Who Said That? More than 2,500 Usable Quotes and Illustrations. Moody Publishers: 1995.

2. You have most probably read a story or watched a movie about a wild-child figure flung by destiny into a jungle where he lives with animals that provide him with nutrition and care. He grows up with these animals and adopts their mode of life, devoid of any external human influence such as parental upbringing or societal culture. Mowgli from The Jungle Book or Tarzan may immediately come to mind. Yet stories about feral children extend further back in time. The Muslim polymath Ibn Tufayl (1105–1185) wrote a philosophical tale of a boy named "Ḥayy Ibn Yaqẓān" who is raised by a doe foster-mother on an equatorial island. Widely popular in Europe during the Enlightenment, Ḥayy Ibn Yaqẓān is a highly influential work. Ḥayy is the only human in the island, surrounded by wild nature and cut off from all signs of civilization. He learns to survive, discovers fire, and devises tools and weapons. He makes sense of the universe on his own terms, without formal instruction. Ḥayy finds God –first by way of independent rational inquiry, then by way of mystical experience. Later, he meets a castaway who takes him to another island inhabited by people having their own culture, language, tradition, religious, legal and commercial codes. Ḥayy, despite having understood them fully, remains unimpressed and returns to his original environment. These tales inspired European philosophers such as Jean Jacques Rousseau and Thomas Hobbes. The wild-child symbolizes the individual who poses existential questions inspired by human nature, and not as a result of circumstances or environmental factors.
"Ibn Tufayl's 'Ḥayy Ibn Yaqẓān': Philosophical Fiction from the 12th Century". On Art and Aesthetics. March 24, 2017.

might arise when you are going through a difficult time and feeling stressed, or in moments of frustration, or simply out of boredom at having to repeat a certain routine. This is why you should consider your actions from a different perspective.

When there is a rational *aim*, any task acquires value and meaning. Simple actions gain significance and are worth the effort when associated with a purpose. If an individual views life as devoid of meaning, this belief would inevitably be reflected in his actions; every breath and movement would have no meaning. Suppose you knowingly enroll at an educational facility which does not provide a graduate certificate upon the completion of your studies. You are aware that there is no future hope of landing a job with this current education but decide to enroll anyway. Would your regular attendance every academic year and examinations be of any value?

Inquiry after the meaning of life is firmly rooted in human history. Even though this concern intensifies when an individual faces a dilemma or misfortune, each individual has an intellectual system which provides an answer to this question. It is worth noting that people's personal characteristics, opinions, forms of expression, modes of conduct, norms and ambitions conform to this system which they have shaped for themselves. Every individual acts as if he is reliant on a certain meaning of life, and all his actions are a reflection of the way he understands the world, himself and the meaning of life.[1]

A person who believes that the acquirement of human values and the adherence to ethical guidelines confer meaning upon life will advance toward self-rectification, while a person who considers pleasure to be the main aim in life will only be concerned with satiating desires.

Those who believe that the universe is a result of random chance and unguided chemical processes can never derive a true meaning from their existence. How could someone who doesn't believe in the Creator be convinced of a purpose-driven

---

1. Adler, Alfred. Understanding Life, p.20.

life? A convict whose guilt has been proven may find a chance for self-contemplation and atonement in prison because he is aware that he is serving a just sentence as punishment for his misdeeds, but an innocent prisoner who has been placed in arbitrary confinement senses the injustice in his imprisonment. Even if he remained for years in his cell and forged ties with his fellow inmates, this forced confinement remains devoid of meaning, while hope in resuming a normal life outside of prison keeps him going. Similarly, whoever views himself as a prisoner of random chance will find no meaning in a life which will end in the dust of the grave.

Proponents of materialism who deny the presence of an Intelligent Designer will remain shackled to an illogical allegation which claims that the universe came into being by chance. If there were no Creator who is aware of all our actions, and if the universe were "a boulder shoved into the desert of existence" as Heidegger states, this implies that life is devoid of purpose. According to this viewpoint, there would be no point in sacrificing oneself for human rights or for freedom as it would be irrational to waste one single, perishable life for the sake of others or future generations. Materialists feel no obligation toward the community they live in[1], and this gives rise to egocentrism where one's own viewpoint and personal interest gain prevalence over all considerations.

Matters are further complicated when belief in a lack of meaning leads to the notion of the absurdity of existence. This concept is evident in "The Myth of Sisyphus", an essay by Albert Camus, which the author himself identifies as a fruitless effort to find meaning in a vast universe with no cause or purpose. This essay argues that life is essentially meaningless although humans continue to try to impose order on existence and to look for answers to unanswerable questions. According to Camus, absurdity arises from the human effort to attain happiness and derive meaning from life even though the natural world constantly evades these attempts. Humans are compared to Sisyphus in Greek mythology, a character condemned for

---

1. Shari'ati, Ali. Al-Insan wal Islam. Dar al-Amir, Beirut: 2007, p.46.

eternity to repeatedly roll a boulder up a hill only to have it roll down again once it reaches the top. Despite his painful exertions, Sisyphus has no choice but to rejoice in his toil.

This, according to Camus, symbolizes the individual's persistent struggle against the absurdity of life even though humans might rejoice in their state. Like Sisyphus, humans can't help but continue to ask after the meaning of existence, only to see their answers tumble back down.[1]

Pessimistic existentialism does not stop there. The book *Nausea* by the French philosopher and novelist Jean-Paul Sartre is an expression of the meaningless of life. *Nausea* is written in diary form and narrates the recurring feelings of revulsion that overcome Roquentin, a young historian, as he comes to realize the emptiness of existence. Roquentin sits by the seashore, reflecting upon existential questions. The nausea which overcomes Roquentin symbolizes the existential anxiety which accompanies the lack of meaning and value in life. In an indifferent world, without work, love, or friendship to sustain him, he must discover value and meaning within himself.[2] According to Sartre, nausea is a state which emerges from the inability to provide an answer to the essential question: *"Why do I exist?"*[3] This drove Sartre to identify the world as a trivial abode of "idiots", with no purpose whatsoever.

Such negative ideas presented by proponents of pessimist philosophy emanated from their rejection of the Creator, leading to the inevitable loss of meaning and purpose in life. Instead of seeking genuine answers to their concerns, pessimist philosophers formulated theories on the meaninglessness of life, having witnessed the crisis between church and science and the rise of materialist tendencies in Europe in the mid 20th century.

---

1. Stanford Encyclopaedia of Philosophy.
2. Britannica
3. Ashraf, Mohammad. The Worry of the Past, 2020. (Personal blog)

The theory of random chance not only affects personal conduct but also causes acute psychological instability when one convinces himself that s/he is a result of "nothing". Conversely, belief in the existence of the Intelligent Cause leads to a belief in the purposefulness of existence. Faith in God inspires humans with hope, tranquility, joy and a sense of meaning. Even materialists have admitted that regardless of one's stance toward faith, belief in God exerts a positive psychological impact and aids believers in overcoming personal, social and economic crises. This has been proven by several studies on how devout people have fewer symptoms of depression and anxiety, as well as a better ability to cope with stress. I have personally participated in a survey conducted by the Lebanese American University on the psychological impact of belief in God, and the findings have corroborated the above information.

Meaning of Life: Conduct and Destiny

In his essay "Existentialism is a Humanism", Jean-Paul Sartre strove to avoid the stark contradiction between his rejection of divine values and his desire to emphasize human values and principles. If there were no God and no afterlife, people would not be rewarded for their righteous deeds nor would they be punished for their evil actions. The absence of God means the absence of right and wrong, the lack of purposefulness in life, and a general feeling of loss and desolation. When there is no belief in recompense and punishment, who can curb the evil that humans are capable of or convince them to adhere to moral principles? If this worldly life were the sole existence, would there be any point in sacrificing oneself or performing altruistic actions?

The American professor and author William Lane Craig relates the following incident: "A number of years ago, a terrible mid-winter air disaster occurred in which a plane leaving the Washington, D.C., airport smashed into a bridge spanning the Potomac River, plunging its passengers into the icy waters. As the rescue helicopters came, attention was focused on one man who again and again pushed the dangling rope ladder to other passengers rather than be pulled to safety himself. Six times he passed the ladder by. When they came again, he was gone. He had freely given his life that others might live. The whole nation turned its eyes to this man in respect and admiration for the selfless and good act he had performed. And yet, if the atheist is right, that man was not noble-he did the stupidest thing possible. He should have gone for the ladder first, pushed others away, if necessary, in order to survive. But to die for others he did not even know, to give up all the brief existence he would ever have-what for? For the atheist there can be no reason. And yet the atheist, like the rest of us, instinctively reacts with praise for this man›s selfless action. Indeed, one will probably never find an atheist who lives consistently with his system. For a universe without moral accountability and devoid of value is unimaginably terrible."[1]

To further elucidate our point, consider how correct letter formations compose comprehensible words while a change in letter order produces unintelligible words. This also applies to words in a sentence structure; displacement of the subject, verb and object renders a sentence meaningless. Similarly, if we contemplate the universe in a disjointed manner, we may never understand the true meaning of this intricate system. Modern science emphasizes the highly organized structure of the universe and the interconnectivity between its parts, but this may only be rationally explained by the existence of an Intelligent Cause. This belief serves in imbuing life with a purpose, assigning a responsibility to every individual, bolstering psychological well-being, and guiding action in all aspects of life. [2]

---

1. Seachris, Joshua (ed.). Exploring the Meaning of Life: An Anthology and Guide. Wiley-Blackwell: 2012, p.167.

2. A theological understanding of life is distinguished by the following points which are relevant to our discussion:
-It is rationally provable; one may benefit from logic to provide evidence on the theological outlook to life and remove any traces of obscurity.
-It confers life with purpose and meaning, guides believers to the ultimate aim and the path to attain it, and eliminates concepts of emptiness and absurdity.
-It urges believers to action, provides them with energy to reach their objectives, and invokes in them feelings of responsibility.
According to this understanding, God created the entire universe in His wisdom upon

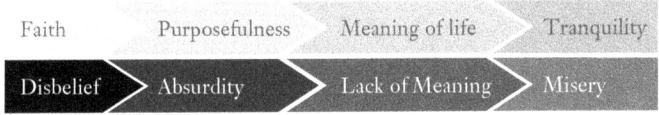

Purpose of Existence

"Why do I exist?"

This question may arise at any moment: when watching a sunset, upon reaching a phase of maturity, while engaging in an intellectual discussion, or during a period of crisis. It rarely surfaces when people are immersed in worldly pleasures because moments of intense joy might lead to satisfaction with life, and in this state humans hardly bother themselves with posing existential questions. If life can be so blissful, why inquire about its purpose? Have you previously heard people wondering why cockroaches or hornets exist, but they don't pose that question regarding roses, birds or sunshine?

The Quest for Perfectibility

A distinguishing characteristic of highly successful people is their knowledge, capacity for achievement, and -quite essentially- their love for their work or area of interest. Can you imagine a brilliant artist who detests painting, an engineer who hates solving mathematical equations, or a sculptor who finds carving tedious? An individual can increase his knowledge and develop his skills, but his spark of interest keeps his energy ablaze. Add talent to the mix and you will find highly appraised works such as the music of Beethoven, the artwork of Picasso, and the novels of Tolstoy and Dostoyevsky.

---

foundations of benevolence and mercy and enabled all creatures to serve their intended purpose. God placed an interconnected system of natural laws and systems, and different aspects of creation, all forming a harmonious whole. Humans can comprehend the beauty of this orderly arrangement. Upon witnessing these aspects of creation and realizing the origin and purpose behind existence, an individual bears his responsibility in life and must strive to display noble qualities such as patience, gratitude, knowledge, awareness and faith, and to be in a state of constant progress.

The love of perfection is inherent in us; we automatically admire the highest degrees of proficiency and excellence and move to achieve them. Muhammad Asad, an Austrian convert to Islam, writes that: "Islam is emphatic in the assertion that man can reach perfection in the earthly, individual life by making full use of all his natural endowments and worldly possibilities. To avoid misunderstandings, the term 'perfection' will have to be defined in the sense it is used here. As long as we have to do with human, biologically limited beings, we cannot possibly consider the idea of 'absolute' perfection, because the Absolute belongs to the realm of Divine attributes alone."[1]

The Infinite Being possesses perfect attributes such as absolute wisdom, power and mercy, and we can conclude that He *wants* these attributes of perfection to be reflected in our finite existence. One who is knowledgeable rejects ignorance, one who is powerful shuns weakness, and one who is benevolent condemns maltreatment. We can say the same of God, the Possessor of Absolute Perfections. He is Perfect and loves to see the marks of perfection on His servants; He is Merciful and wants His servants to wisely display mercy among their fellow creatures; He is Knowledgeable and wants His servants to seek knowledge and acquire wisdom.

One of my friends was enamored with physics. He eagerly awaited physics learning sessions at school, and when he reached university, he chose to major in physics without any hesitation and graduated with exceptionally high honors. His skill in physics was merged with his love for this subject, and he even evaluated people according to their mastery of physics! This captivation awakened in him a love for teaching, to the extent that he offered physics lessons in return for a salary or even for free. He even founded a physics club at his own expense to aid pupils in mastering their skills.

Every true admirer or possessor of a form of perfection wishes to see that quality reflected in others or to aid them

---

1. Asad, Muhammad. Islam at the Crossroads. The Other Press. Kuala Lumpur: 2005, p.10.

in acquiring it. When we declare that God is the possessor of the attributes of perfection, this involves aiding His servants to achieve perfection qualities such as knowledge[1], mercy, and competence.

From the preceding clarification, we may understand one facet regarding the purpose of existence. Creation is a manifestation of several divine attributes of perfection, most significantly the attribute of mercy. Through His compassion, God created humans and guided them toward qualities of perfection. "There is a correlation between divine perfections and creaturely ones. Perfections that are found in the world are the effects of God's properties. Since God is the origin, which gives being to all things that come to exist, things that come to exist do so in accordance with the goodness and the perfection of their source. Avicenna clearly states that not only do things that come to exist follow the divine being and perfections, but that the manner of their existence also follows the divine goodness and perfection. Thus, the perfections that creatures display are the reflection of the divine goodness and perfection"[2].

Purpose of Creation: Reaping Personal Benefits?

In our personal experience, our actions are linked to our needs; we sit down to rest, we work to achieve financial security, we eat to satiate our hunger, and so forth. Our needs motivate us to take action. But how can we explain God's actions?

One of the Names of God is al-Ghanī, the Self-Sufficient who needs nothing and no one. Therefore, it is more accurate when inquiring about the meaning of existence to use the term *"wisdom behind creation"* rather than *"aim of creation"* because the latter may indicate the presence of a need which requires

---

1. "Perhaps the most important of the divine attributes that human beings manifest are knowledge and understanding. Certainly, as Franz Rosenthal has shown in Knowledge Triumphant, no religious tradition places more emphasis upon the importance of knowledge than Islam."
Chittick, William. The Islamic Concept of Human Perfection.

2. Acar, Rahim. Talking About God and Talking About Creation: Avicenna's and Thomas Aquinas' Positions. Brill: 2005, p.29.

accomplishment. The various aspects of creation which we witness are *reflections* of the perfection attributes of the Creator and a result of His wise actions, and not *aims* which God needs to fulfill.

To clarify this more, consider the following example. You perform an action with a desired outcome in mind; you visit the grocery store to buy necessary household products, and you occupy yourself with recreational activities for enjoyment. You have an aim which you want to achieve. Some people spend money for personal benefit such as wealthy candidates who pay large sums of money during election campaigns with the aim of winning. Conversely, there are generous individuals who spend money out of their altruistic concern for human welfare and with no expectation of recompense[1].

But can you ask what do parents *aim* at when they care for their children? A mother provides unconditional love for her child, deprives herself of sleep for his welfare, and endures the mental load and stressful demands of motherhood. If you ask a mother what she aims at from caring for her child and hint that she is doing so for her own personal interest or to ensure her welfare when she grows up, she will laugh at such an absurd suggestion. Mothers are not bound by narrow self-interests or material aims, nor do they expect anything in return from their children. The compassion which God planted in the hearts of mothers motivates them to endure emotional stress and physical exertion to ensure the well-being of their offspring. The immense mercy a mother displays toward her children is only a small sign of the all-encompassing mercy of God.

God loves you, nurtures you, guides you, and bestows His grace upon you in so many ways. He is not in need of you, nor does he derive any gain from your existence. Creation is a reflection of His wisdom, mercy, and power, and does not arise

---

1. Take Hatem al-Tai for example, a pre-Islamic Arabian figure known for his extreme generosity. When visited by guests, he would provide their needs for the first three days without asking them a single question. If they requested milk, he slaughtered a she-camel to feed them, and if they praised him for his hospitality he distributed his wealth upon them. The Arabic proverb "more generous than Hatem" is used today.

from a need or desire to seek a certain advantage. Hence, it is more accurate to ask about the wisdom behind divine actions.

PURPOSE OF HUMAN EXISTENCE

Why did God create humans? In light of the previous elucidation, it is clear that creation is a reflection of divine attributes (especially all-embracing divine mercy and love). Since humans are part of this awe-inducing tapestry of creation, they are recipients of divine grace. Yet humans occupy a central position in the cosmos, to the extent that the following fundamental question is bound to arise: *What is the purpose of human existence? How can we accomplish God's plan?*

A Glimpse into Human Capacities

The stages of human development, from the neonatal stage to infancy, childhood, adolescence and adulthood, are distinguished by advancement in mental competence and the ability to perform. In what follows are descriptions of human capacities:

Human capacities are numerous and diverse. God endowed humans with capacities which are numerous. Ethically, humans can adopt moral principles such as honesty, generosity, patience and humility, while they can socially demonstrate tolerance, cooperation and mutual respect toward one another. On the personal level, humans have the ability to improve certain aspects of their personalities such as self-confidence, adaptability, and consistency. Developmental psychology studies human growth and development, and this includes physical, cognitive, social, intellectual, perceptual and emotional growth.

The American psychologist Howard Gardner proposed the theory of multiple intelligences where he divided intelligences into eight types: linguistic, logical-mathematical, naturalist, spatial, musical, bodily-kinesthetic, interpersonal and intrapersonal[1].

Human capacities vary in degree. Humans collectively possess capacities and intelligences, but these are present in individuals in varying degrees and are liable to further development and utilization. If someone senses a deficiency in a certain capacity or competence, s/he can exert an effort to enhance it. At the same time, diversity in skills gives them value and makes the world a more interesting place. Some people excel at poetry while others are clever at math or a certain sport. Imagine that everyone possessed the same skill in painting, what value would artwork maintain? Common capacities give us a glimpse into the justice of God while talents give us an image of the diverse beauty of creation.

The Spiritual and Material Composites

Humans combine two aspects, the spiritual and the material. Perfectibility is not associated with one's external appearance but with moral development. Even though attention should be provided to healthy nutrition and physical activities, but the center of concern should be the spiritual aspect.

Every human being will reach a peak in bodily ability but will inevitably face physical decline, and this emphasizes the temporal nature of the material aspect. Athletes retire at a certain age when they are past their peak performance. With age, visits to doctors for check-ups become a part of normal life. Humans desire to stop the toll of time on their bodies, to somehow impede ageing, and have attempted to do so in various ways: "Backed by governments, businesses, academics, and investors in an industry worth $110 billion –and estimated to be worth $610 billion by 2025- scientists have spent decades attempting to harness the power of genomics and artificial intelligence to find a way to prevent or even reverse ageing. But an unprecedented study has now confirmed that we probably

---

1. Gardner, Howard. Multiple Intelligences. Basic Books: 2008.

cannot slow the rate at which we get older because of biological constraints."[1]

Ageing is a gradual, continuous process. Strength and physical robustness are followed by frailty and decline in bodily functions. Sooner or later, wrinkles will appear on your face, your hair will start to gray, and the chores which once seemed so easy to carry out will require an extra effort. The material aspect is heading toward decay, but the spiritual aspect is immersed in immortality. This is why the pursuit of perfection should be oriented toward the immaterial aspect. The purpose of human existence is to transform capacities into fixed perfection traits which make up one's personality and inspire his/her actions.

Intellect and Willpower

Different philosophies have proposed various perceptions on human perfection, varying from the satiation of physical desires to the advancement of personal interest. However, when we consider human perfection, we must pay attention to two points which are relevant here.

a) Acquiring knowledge of perfection is done by the **intellect**;

b) Human perfection is a manifestation of the traits and values adopted by an upright human. Wealth, physical prowess, fame, or noble lineage are not indicators of human dignity; rather it is the adoption of moral principles and virtuous actions which defines a human being. This may not be achieved without **willpower,** the control over your impulses and actions and determination to remain steadfast.

Therefore, the uniqueness of human beings lies in their possession of intellect and willpower. When it comes to willpower: "Ask people to name their greatest personal strengths, and they'll often credit themselves with honesty,

---

1. Hill. Amelia. "Ageing Process is Unstoppable, Finds Unprecedented Study". The Guardian. June 17, 2021.

kindness, humor, creativity, bravery, and other virtues –even modesty. But not self-control. It came in dead last among the virtues being studied by researchers who have surveyed more than one million people around the world. Of the two dozen 'character strengths' listed in the researchers' questionnaire, self-control was the one that people were least likely to recognize in themselves. Conversely, when people were asked about their failings, a lack of self-control was at the top of the list."[1]

Humans are embroiled in a constant everyday clash between good and evil, justice and oppression, truth and falsehood. They need willpower, patience, and fortitude to choose what is right and refuse what is wrong, to cling to values and reject vices, and to act morally even if it contradicts personal interests. Through willpower, one controls behavior and enhances his diverse capacities to achieve perfection. In this manner can the purpose of creation be fulfilled: to come into possession of qualities of perfection -such as generosity, patience, gratitude, loyalty, bravery and compassion- and to outwardly express them out of your own free will.

As previously mentioned, attributes of perfection belong to God, and humans must strive to adopt these attributes and translate them into action. Therefore, one must emulate divine attributes and display justice, knowledge, generosity, mercy toward the downtrodden, and retribution against oppressors. These attributes are criteria for conduct which we should constantly strive for. As divine attributes are boundless, one lives in a constant and continuous state to fulfill these attributes in himself. The more a person adopts these attributes and applies them in life, s/he fulfills the purpose of creation.[2] "According to the Quran, God created humans out of dust and clay by blowing into them of His divine spirit, thus making humans capable of being God's viceroy (*khalifa*) on earth (Quran 2:30). Having created Adam and breathed His spirit (*ruh*) into him,

---

1. Baumeister, Roy; Tierney, John. Willpower: Rediscovering the Greatest Human Strength. The Penguin Press: 2011.
2. Mujaz Usul al-Din, p.180.

God granted Adam (and his progeny) the faculty of knowledge, conceptual thinking, a conscience, free choice, and the ability to progress toward human perfection."[1]

It remains important to adopt a careful balance when it comes to attributes. For instance, God is merciful but inflicts his wrath upon the wrongdoers, he rewards righteous servants with eternal bliss but punishes the wicked with a severe torment. Hence, one should be careful when applying these attributes as different incidents dictate varying modes of conduct. For instance, peaceful individuals are worthy of kindness but oppressors should be met with punishment; certain individuals deserve to be forgiven and granted another chance while clemency toward transgressors who will act more viciously after being pardoned is unacceptable. Different circumstances require a careful consideration of conduct. This entails a balance in attributes, and wisdom in behavior. Strong willpower prevents us from being carried away by our personal desires and acting in a manner unsuitable in the situation at hand.

How can capacities be transformed into actual personality traits?

Regardless of a person's belief in life after death, it is universally acknowledged that our life on earth is riddled with hardship and pain, and that wishes come true after the exertion of strenuous efforts. Similarly, a person needs to strive diligently to translate perfection traits into conduct. Life is like a training ground where participants undergo difficult physical exercises, endure harsh conditions, sleep on the bare ground, and maneuver risky geographical terrain.

One of the most important human traits is freewill. You have the choice to select a certain alternative or to perform a certain action without restraint. When you choose to be generous and act accordingly, you are a benevolent person; when you bear

---

1. Coward, Harold. The Perfectibility of Human Nature in Eastern and Western Thought. State university of New York Press: 2008, p.82.

misfortunes, provocations and hardship with fortitude, you are a patient person.

What is certain is that numerous factors influence a person's beliefs and behavior such as one's family, friends, and school. This influence, however, is not over-powering nor does it deprive humans of their free will. Socialization is a concept in social psychology which refers to the process by which individuals acquire social skills, beliefs, values, and conduct necessary to function effectively in society or in a particular group. Most sociologists and psychologists have acknowledged the varying degrees of influence which social structures exert, but agree that they do not nullify a person's free will.

While you are reading this book, you are free to continue reading or to close it and put it aside. You choose to perform acts of worship, you decide on a certain major in university, and you determine where you want to live or work. You have free choice.

Through voluntary actions, humans can reach perfection, become responsible for their choices, and are held accountable for their actions. Human dignity rests on the ability to make free choices. If human actions were mechanically pre-established, humans would be no different than animals that act solely according to their instincts

There is a close relationship between resolve and free will. For instance, when you choose to study diligently instead of wasting your time and procrastinating, you enforce your determination to pursue knowledge. Similarly, when you react calmly you strengthen your fortitude. When you choose to perform good instead of evil, your resolve is strengthened. Implementation of freewill by performing praiseworthy strengthens your resolve. If you lacked freewill, your determination would know no improvement

Take the following story for example. Demosthenes was a famous orator in ancient Greece who debated the most prominent statesmen and judges at the ripe age of twenty. Demosthenes was born into a wealthy Athenian family. When he was seven, his father died leaving his estate for his son in the trust of three guardians. According to Demosthenes' own account, the guardians mismanaged and defrauded the estate to the point that when he turned eighteen, he received almost nothing. Demosthenes devoted the next several years to recovering his property. He launched a series of trials against these immoral guardians to recover his patrimony. In the course of these trials, he gained a reputation as a successful speaker.[1]

But matters were not so smooth at the beginning. According to Plutarch, "when he first addressed himself to the people, he was met with great discouragements, and was derided for his strange and uncouth style… Besides, he had, it seems, a weakness in his voice, a perplexed and indistinct utterance and a shortness of breath which, by breaking and disjointing his sentences, much obscured the sense and meaning of what he spoke. So that in the end, being quite disheartened, he forsook the assembly".[2]

Demosthenes did not give up and chose the hard path. He constructed a place to study underground where he practiced. He also improved his vocal skills by speaking with pebbles in his mouth on the seashore over the roar of the waves. Demosthenes was able to defend his right through rhetoric and returned his lost inheritance. He is recognized as the greatest of ancient Greek orators, and was even able to rouse Athens in opposition to Philip of Macedon.

While it is true that humans are born with different capacities, each person has the ability and willpower to alter his personal traits. If you have a certain fear, you can muster the courage to overcome it, and if you notice an unfavorable personal trait you can strive to change it. When you realize the power of free choice, you can transform challenges into opportunities.

---

1. Gagarin, Micheal. The Oratory of Classical Greece: Demosthenes, SPEECHES 27-38. Translated by Douglas MacDowell. University of Texas Press. 2004, p.3.
2. Edited by Eliot, Charles. Plutarch's Lives. Cosimo Inc. 2009: p, 201.

Self-improvement is a personal choice and an achievable goal. The purpose of correctional facilities and institutions for social integration is the rehabilitation of delinquents, but if an individual refuses to alter his conduct, then no social worker or institute would be able to effectively aid him. Some individuals might attribute their failures and shortcomings to "unfortunate circumstances" or "bad luck", but experience has proven that hundreds of individuals have overcome their adverse conditions.

Take Clyde Beasley for example. He spent 11 years behind bars on drug charges. One night in prison, he was barred from attending a golf match he had been anticipating. After spending hours in a state of disappointment, he came up with the idea to construct a small golf set on a table. He spent years designing a new model and presented it to a gaming industry which adopted his idea. In a few years, Clyde Beasley amassed great wealth –legally- and became a successful entrepreneur.

Success stories are numerous and inspiring. Wallace Johnson, co-founder of the Holiday Inns hotel chain, was fired from work during the Great Depression. He relates his story as follows: "When I was forty years old, I worked in a sawmill. One morning the boss told me, 'You're Fired!' I was depressed and discouraged and felt like the world caved in on me. It was during the depression, and my wife and I greatly needed the small wages I had been earning. So I went home and told my wife what happened and she said, 'What are you going to do now?' So I replied, 'I'm going to mortgage our little home and go into the building business.' My first venture was the construction of two small buildings. Within five years I was a multi-millionaire! Today, if I could locate the man who fired me, I would sincerely thank him for what he did. At the time it happened, I didn't understand why I was fired. Later though, I saw that it was God's unerring and wondrous plan to get me into the way of His choosing!" [1]

---

1. Crone, Billy. The Character of God. 2017, p.147.

The Worldly Life and the Hereafter

This worldly life is the arena where humans willingly transform their capacities into action and strengthen their determination. This world is not a place for leisure and relaxation, but a test where we prove our mettle. It is where we may develop positive qualities regardless of age, time period, geographical boundaries and circumstances, and where we bear the responsibility for attaining perfection, intensifying our efforts despite the hardship we face.

Years will swiftly pass by. Even if they are fraught with difficulties, the afterlife awaits where righteous souls will reap their rewards. There are two joys in pursuing this path, one in the worldly life where every sincere step toward earning God's pleasure is a cause for rejoicing, and one in the afterlife where one shall gain a divine reward.

"We know that with your weak legs you will never be able to accomplish the journey- in a hundred thousand years you would not complete even one stage of the journey. But when you make the effort and collapse and fall down, unable to take another step, then God's loving grace will carry you." [1]

-Rumi

Achievements require hard work, even tending your garden requires commitment. It is strange how humans strive toward comfort in this worldly life and the acquirement of material gains which last for a fleeting period of time, but neglect their eternal abode. The bliss which awaits us for eternity is an impetus which drives us toward sublime spiritual goals.

You might exert an effort in this life but not necessarily achieve your aims, but heavenly recompense is certain and this generates inner tranquility. This outlook to the hereafter casts difficulties in a different light. Predicaments and obstacles are no longer a cause for sorrow but a means for spiritual

---

1. Helminski, Kabir; Helminski, Camille. The Rumi Daybook. Shambhala: 2012, p.82.

refinement. The hardship we face is an inherent blessing; thorns protect roses, night heralds the arrival of dawn.

Why didn't God create perfect humans?

Upon witnessing oppression, warfare, and injustice in the world, one wonders about human nature. Thinkers such as Plato, Hesiodos, and Thomas Moore speculated about Utopia -a place of ideal perfection whose inhabitants enjoy peace and optimum conditions- but the reality on earth presented a stark contrast leading them to realize the complexity of such a concept.

Why didn't God create us perfect?

First, the purpose of creation lies in human attainment of perfection, and God's attributes are the most manifest representation of perfection. Knowledge, wisdom, and mercy are divine traits and so is freedom of choice. An individual is not able to gain perfection without possessing freewill. Conscious positive actions deserve praise and recognition. For example, a man who rises from humble origins and attains wealth through diligent work is praised in society, but this admiration does not extend to his son who was born into a privileged family.

Second, choice has value. Attainment of positive attributes through coercion does not lead to perfection since a person has no choice in the matter. For instance, a person who offers impoverished people financial aid wholeheartedly differs from someone who is compelled to give charity or someone who does so to promote his personal image. The donated sum might be the same, but the nature of the action makes all the difference.

Suppose two individuals are facing a dilemma. One of them seeks divine aid and asks God to help him react with wisdom and patience, without hurting anyone's feelings. The other, however, is incapable of controlling his reactions and prefers to lock himself in his room to calm down and refrains from mingling with people. The former is stronger because he is able to control his emotions and temper. Through freedom of choice, humans are able to reach an elevated status. When a person faces two choices, evil and good, and chooses the path of virtue regardless of temptations, s/he can reach a rank higher than angels.

Third, willpower is a distinguishing human quality, and therefore everything which strengthens willpower gains value. Steadfastness during the inner struggle between good and evil fortifies determination. For instance, there are two ways to quit smoking: either by personal choice -even though this is a daunting task- or by trying nicotine replacement therapy. The first method requires more effort because it involves personal resilience, avoiding smoking triggers, and dealing with the negative side-effects of nicotine-withdrawal.

Fourth, we attribute significance to things in concurrence with their value and the amount of effort required to attain them. The more we labor and struggle emotionally and physically to achieve something, the more precious is our achievement.A person who exerts time and effort to gain something prizes it more than someone who received it with no pain and takes its presence for granted.

Eternal bliss is a result of conscious acts of virtue and the voluntary adoption of commendable attributes. The reward in the hereafter differs from one person to another based on willpower. The harder the choices you make, the stronger your resolve becomes. The stronger the resolve, the higher the rank in heaven. For instance, one might have to choose between safeguarding a hefty endowment or betraying trust for personal gain. Or one might decide between showing mercy to someone who wronged him or seeking revenge.

A person's fate in the hereafter is hinged on his willpower. Many people are unmindful of the cause of their existence and fail in transforming their inner capacities into fruitful conduct. Such is the state of life; some will soar, others will fall. Suppose there is a remote rural area with a newly built school. The person in charge of this school is well aware that children's capabilities differ in degree; some will gain high grades and display a penchant for learning while others will fall short of success. This, however, does not prevent him from including all the children in the school program, without losing hope in them. He strives to provide all of them with education without discrimination. Those who receive knowledge but neglect their studies will only have themselves to blame.

What is the Purpose of Hell?

You might have asked yourself: If the divine plan is for humans to reach perfection, then what is the purpose of hell? To answer this inquiry, we should consider the following: How can we reconcile God's love toward humanity with the concept of hell?

a) In view of God's mercy, His endowment of humans with the intellect and the *fitra* (predisposition toward belief), and His dispatch of messengers and prophets to guide mankind, we understand that God wants humans to turn to Him.

b) At the same time, it is important to note that punishment of offenders is in itself a form of justice. Would it be logical to grant a corrupt person the same reward as an upright individual, or to overlook the misconduct of oppressors? Could it be possible to equate a drug dealer who destroys the lives of hundreds of juveniles with a person who strives for social welfare?

The Holy Quran refers to this basic principle in the following verse:

"Or should we treat those who believe and do righteous deeds like the corrupters on earth? Or should We treat the pious like the wicked?"

(Quran 38:28)

c) There are man-made rules and regulations which members of society abide by. For instance, students accept their institution's grading system, while citizens accept the penal code. There are also natural laws where every cause has an effect: Drinking water quenches thirst, sharp objects wound, and fire burns. Punishment which awaits wrongdoers doesn't fall into the first category.

Every sin has a fire which we don't see with our eyes in this world but which will become manifest in the hereafter when veils are removed. Punishment in that realm is a result of one's actions and characteristics. On the other hand, a moment of sincere repentance may alter a human's fate. The gate to repentance is forever open, with no need for an intermediary or a special ceremony.

It is also important to note that a human is punished in the hereafter in proportionality to the divine proof he received. A person's rejection of divine guidance after it has reached him causes a sharper downfall. There is a rule in theology which states that whoever receives more divine guidance and abides by it shall reach higher perfection, but if he faces this guidance with rejection or failure to act devoutly, he shall bear the results of his actions more acutely. From this, we can understand why the severest punishment awaits Pharoah and his followers.

- *"But when Our signs came to them, plain to see, they said, 'This is obvious magic.'*

And they denied them, though their souls acknowledged them, out of injustice and haughtiness. So, see how was the end of the corrupters!"
(Quran 27:13-14)

- *"And on the day when the Hour shall come to pass [it will be said]: 'Make the People of Pharaoh enter the severest torment.'"*
(Quran 40:46)

Pathway to Perfection

How can we attain spiritual refinement and eternal bliss? How can we transform our capacities into perfection traits?

There are two means to achieve this. The first is reliance on the intellect by carefully considering moral qualities. Intellect which is in harmony with the *fitra* and unaffected by personal interests concludes the value of qualities such as justice, honesty and loyalty as opposed to oppression, deceit, and treachery. For proper judgment, intellect requires knowledge of:

a-Individual and social perfection, and placement of personal interests aside.

b-Complementarity between the earthly life and the hereafter, taking into account that actions in this world are reflected in the afterlife.

c-Soul and body welfare, without neglecting one of these two aspects. In many modern societies, the spiritual aspect is largely ignored even though local populations enjoy financial stability. This is due to allotting importance to the material aspect and disregarding the spiritual one. But it is noticeable how in developed wealthy societies, many suffer from unhappiness. Depression rates around the world vary according to a nation's affluence, with the highest income countries -including the U.S.- reporting the highest levels of depression, a study shows.[1]

The second way is to follow the *Sharia* which governs all aspects of a believer's life. God guides humans to true perfection, and did not create us and leave us lost and alone. Therefore, following the *Sharia* is the means to attain perfection. According to Rumi: "The *Sharia* (law) is like a lamp showing the path. Without it, the path cannot be trodden. The path you tread upon is the Tariqa. The destination you reach is the *Haqiqa* (reality)."[2]

A believer is confident that there is an inherent wisdom in every ruling. Religious obligations ensure benefits while

---

1. McMillen, Matt. "Richer Countries Have Higher Depression Rates: Study Shows U.S. Has World's Second Highest Depression Rate". WebMD. July 26, 2011.
2. Demmrich, Sarah; Riegel, Ulrich. Western and Eastern Perspectives on Religion and Religiosity. Waxmann: 2020, p.50.

prohibitions shield us from moral and material harm. If a certain matter includes a portion of good and evil, those two aspects are weighed and a ruling is issued accordingly. Therefore, we need to abide by the intellect and the Sharia to proceed on the path to perfection.

Chapter four
The Human Need for Religion

The previous chapters aimed at elucidating the origin of life and the purpose of existence by using logical reasoning and drawing on scientific findings. At this point it is pertinent to present the Islamic outlook to life. Religion is the message of the Creator to His rational creatures, and hence it is incumbent upon every individual to contemplate this message to discover its meanings. The first step is to logically determine that the message you have received is from God, and this is achieved by mental reasoning. In this context, this chapter proceeds to clarify the significance of religion and to present evidence on the most complete religion.

What is Religion?

There are several definitions for religion, but we can state the following here: Religion is a message which you believe in rationally or traditionally or experientially, and which forms a vital connection between you and your Creator. It exerts an influence over your emotions and governs your actions through an epistemological, spiritual and behavioral system.

When you travel to foreign countries and go sightseeing, you notice the local architecture, shops, ancient ruins, forts, old districts, markets, and natural landscape. A certain feature may be present in a country but absent in another, but you will never find a city or a community without a place of worship.

Many philosophers and intellectuals believed that religious belief would become obsolete in modern times. "Marx, like Auguste Comte and a number of other intellectuals in the nineteenth century, believed that wherever modern science and technology penetrated, religion was doomed. It might persist for a while, but it could have no real vitality left in the modern world; its last spasmodic struggling would soon be ended and it would lie still. Such has not been the case. Religion survives the spread of science, and scientists are among those who continue to adhere to religion."[1] Contrary to their "predictions", it is evident that no matter the trends of irreligiosity in a certain region, humans will always feel pulled toward religion.

1. The Need for Religion

Some people are inclined toward religiosity due to their religious background, while others feel compelled to adhere to religious practices due to the religious environment they live in or out of fear of ostracism. However, it is vital to overcome old-fashioned concepts regarding religion and to reach an understanding of its true meaning. Religion is not a shackling force, nor a hindrance, nor should it be adhered to only traditionally and without profound contemplation. Religion is a system of belief and devotional practices by which one may understand the meaning of existence, satisfy the intrinsic *fitra* which drives the soul toward spirituality, and discover the rules of conduct which one must abide by and through which life becomes balanced. "To be spiritually balanced, an individual must have elements of both *'jamali'* and *'jalali'* attributes in one's life. In other words, there must be expansion as well as contraction. There must be compassion as well as justice. There must be ease as well as vigor. There must be peace as well as struggle. There must be forgiveness as well as accountability. There must be love as well as logic."[2]

Some parents or communities present religion to youth in an unconvincing manner. Due to their lack of sufficient knowledge and poor communication skills, they demonstrate religion in a distorted or even fear-inducing manner. It only gets worse when they falsely attribute to religion ideas which contradict logic. This might plant aversion in the hearts of young adults toward religion and drive them away from it. But if religion is presented in a true light, with wisdom and kindness, and as a human need, people would inevitably find

---

1. Ling, Trevor. The Persistence of Religion. In: Karl Marx and Religion. Palgrave, London: 1980.

2. Whitehouse, Anab. The Nature of the Sufi Path. The Interrogative Imperative Institute: 2018: p.124.

themselves inclined toward it. Let us put aside parental and societal pressure and overlook traditional adherence to religion, asking objectively: Is religion an imposed social phenomenon or an essential human need?

A. Basic Human Needs

Social psychology examines human needs. In his book Motivation and Personality, the American psychologist Abraham Maslow discusses the hierarchy of human needs1.His theory suggests that people have a number of basic needs that must be met before people move up the hierarchy to pursue more social, emotional, and self-actualizing needs.

The first level is the fulfillment of physiological needs which are biological requirements for human survival, such as air, food, drink, shelter, clothing, warmth, and sleep. If these needs are not satisfied, the human body cannot function optimally. Then come safety needs; once an individual's physiological needs are satisfied, the needs for security and safety become necessary. After physiological and safety needs have been fulfilled, the third level of human needs is social and involves feelings of belongingness. The need for interpersonal relationships motivates behavior. Examples include friendship, intimacy, trust, and acceptance, and receiving and giving affection and love. Esteem needs are the fourth level in Maslow's hierarchy -which Maslow classified into two categories: (i) esteem for oneself (dignity, achievement, mastery, independence) and (ii) the desire for reputation or respect from others (e.g., status, prestige). Self-actualization needs are the highest level in Maslow's hierarchy, and refer to the realization of a person's potential, self-fulfillment, seeking personal growth and peak experiences. A desire "to become everything one is capable of becoming". [2]

Through our intuition, we may differentiate between two types of categories: physiological/material needs and spiritual/

---

1. Maslow, Abraham. Motivation and Personality. Harper and Row: 1954, p.127.

2. Rodulfo, Juan. Why Maslow? P.27-28

psychological needs. The former refers to the satisfaction of natural instincts such as thirst and hunger and is also reflected in the preoccupation with the self, such as tending carefully to the outer appearance and pursuing wealth and fame. This fuels the ego, linking the individual to his material presence on earth. It may be stated that the greater portion of Maslow's exposition lies in this category. Concurrently, one's humanity and elevation of spirit is manifest in abstract concepts such as love, longing, sacrifice, forgiveness and mercy.

Perhaps children may be considered the most prominent example on genuine psychological human needs because they enjoy a purity that adults lack (due to years of influence by parents, school, the social environment, and mainstream media). Elderly individuals exhibit this tendency to a certain degree due to the fading of secondary desires such as the pursuit of wealth, status and procreation while maintaining initial needs.

Children sense their weakness and needs and thus seek refuge in their parents, but when they grow older and build physical strength, they might develop a feeling of self-importance. However, when an individual faces trouble or becomes frail, s/he senses once again the need to turn to a great and capable power. This innate inclination –the *fitra*- drives humans towards the Creator. Humans naturally strive toward high degrees of proficiency and excellence –power, knowledge, strength, wealth- but it is noteworthy that when a person reaches a certain triumph or achievement, he yearns for more. This urge emanates from the *fitra* toward the supreme and unlimited perfection: God.

Religiosity is a common trait that anthropologists study in their examination of the sacred. Religion is a need because it satisfies the human *fitra*, the everlasting quest for a connection with the divine in humans. Einstein made a reference to a "cosmic religious sense" which he described as follows: "This is hard to make clear to those who do not experience it… The individual feels the vanity of human desires and aims, and the nobility and marvelous order which are revealed in nature and in the world of thought."

B. Religion Provides Meaningfulness

Not only is religion a human need, but it also satisfies the basic human instinct of self-preservation, a major need in humans. Humans yearn for the prolongation of existence, but experience inner turmoil as they struggle to reconcile their finite existence with their inherent longing for infinitude. According to Paul Tillich, one must personally face the challenge of non-being: "The anxiety of fate and death is most basic, most universal, and inescapable. All attempts to argue it away are futile."[1]

Every living human is certain that s/he will die someday, and this concept produces concern to the extent that Sartre considers that life loses its meaning the moment we stop believing in immortality. Individuals who are familiar with death such as gravediggers may declare that they are not particularly scared of death, but when, according to Sartre, death becomes a personal threat, one begins to sense the anxiety of nonbeing and the passage of one's existence into forgetfulness.

The meaning of life depends on endurance of existence. What point lies in the efforts to improve mankind, campaign for world peace, and sacrifice for humanity if everything will end in decay? Religion is the only savior of the need for self-preservation. Monotheistic religions perceive life as stages which a human traverses before moving on to the hereafter. In this vein, death is not the cessation of being but a journey. This renders life meaningful, confers tranquility upon the soul, and emphasizes responsibility. Religion is the only means to fully gratify the instinct of self-preservation, while all materialist philosophies stand powerless in the face of this challenge.

---

1. Dash, Michael; Jones, Bridget. Perspectives on Language and Literature, 1985.

C. A Safe Haven

A heart monitor records the strength and timing of your heart's activity. The lines rise and fall on the screen to depict your heart rate. Such is the state of life on earth. There are constant changes: in seasons, planting and harvesting, the ebb and flow of the ocean, health and sickness, life and death. These changes are like the lines on a heart monitor, continuously rising, and falling. We drift between pain and joy, worry and comfort, turmoil and tranquility.

During difficult times, some factors offer solace such as loving family members, but an individual's personal bond with God provides the greatest source of comfort, inspiring a believer with hope and strength in the face of all hardships. Have you noticed how in a moment of distress or fear, you seek refuge in God, your heart pounding and calling His Name.

"Those who have believed and whose hearts are assured by the remembrance of Allah. Verily, by the remembrance of Allah are hearts assured."

(Quran 13:28)

D. Religion as A Law-Enforcer

Developed countries adopt two methods to preserve security and curb crime rates. The first method is to impose strict laws which apply to all citizens, unhindered by bribery or favoritism, where every guilty person is held accountable for his crime. The second method is to focus on education with the aim of forming a generation which willingly respects rules and regulations, therefore avoiding resort to threats of punishment. This method is critical as it is not possible to guarantee the discipline of all citizens even with the prospect of severe penalties, and therefore instruction is essential for ensuring behavior which adheres to the law.

Religiosity plays a vital role in bolstering these two methods through "personal surveillance". A believer who is convinced of the sinfulness of breaking the law, theft, murder and treachery will avoid such actions, even if there was no one around. There might be no human eyes watching you at a certain moment, but God is aware of all your actions and ever-watchful of that which you do.

"Indeed, from Allah nothing is hidden in the earth nor in heaven."

(Quran 3:5)

Belief in God promotes self-discipline. In the United States, police departments benefit immensely from the services of chaplains. Chaplains improve the overall functioning of law enforcement through involvement in correctional facilities, community-police relations, crisis intervention, and officer and department well-being[1]. When inner religious restraint is accompanied with an outer punishment system, results are more fruitful.

E. Discipline and Willpower

We previously highlighted the importance of free will as an essential human trait. You can choose between good and evil, success or failure. Strengthening willpower leads to achievement. Religiosity highly contributes to the development of willpower as it imposes rulings which regulate action (and which benefit humans). For instance, prayer is performed at prescribed times, fasting regulates times of food consumption, and paying zakat controls one's attachment to money.

F. Religion Provides a Comprehensive Worldview

The religious worldview is distinguished by complementary elements which other worldviews lack:

It relies upon mental reasoning which involves rational preambles and conclusions.

It does not evade questions nor does it fail in presenting solutions to complex issues.

---

1. Braswell, Richard; Steinkopf, Bryan; Beamer, Angela. "Law Enforcement Chaplains: Defining Their Roles". Law Enforcement Bulletin. Nov.9, 2016.

It is inclusive, encompassing the spiritual and physical aspect, the individual and the social sphere, the worldly life and the hereafter. This ensures its continuity regardless of changes in place, time or circumstances.

It has a logical, emotional, and behavioral aspect, and is not restricted to mere theorization.

It connects the past and the struggle of the prophets with the present, and paves the way for the future, maintaining the endeavor of truth and virtue.

It correlates people's worldly deeds with the hereafter, thus placing a responsibility upon every individual for his actions and urging humans to compete in righteous deeds to attain elevated ranks in the hereafter.

2. Discovering Religion

The religion of truth is accompanied with indisputable logical proof, preventing manipulators and profiteers from exploiting the pure *fitra* of humans to advance their personal interests and aims by false allegations. When proving the authenticity of a religion, it is critical to examine the aspects pertaining to its leader.

We may apply the following principles to the critical question: Why should I believe in Islam? Is it the mode of life which allows me to acquire knowledge of God, to understand the purpose of my existence, and to fulfill my responsibility in life?

A. Divine Heralds

We may corroborate the prophecy of Prophet Muhammad (ṣ) by referring to divine tidings of his advent. Believers in the messages of divinely-inspired prophets such as Moses and Jesus are the ones to mainly benefit from this principle. The tidings in the holy books which God sent to these prophets is a guiding point for later generations.

The Quran mentions:

"Muhammad is the Messenger of Allah; and those with him are forceful against the disbelievers, merciful among themselves. You see them bowing and prostrating [in prayer], seeking bounty from Allah and [His] pleasure. Their mark is on their faces from the trace of prostration. That is their description in the Torah. And their description in the Gospel is as a plant which produces its offshoots and strengthens them so they grow firm and stand upon their stalks, delighting the sowers - so that Allah may enrage by them the disbelievers. Allah has promised those who believe and do righteous deeds among them forgiveness and a great reward."

(Quran 48:29)

"And [mention] when Jesus, the son of Mary, said, 'O children of Israel, indeed I am the messenger of Allah to you confirming what came before me of the Torah and bringing good tidings of a messenger to come after me, whose name is Ahmad.' But when he came to them with clear proofs, they said, 'This is obvious magic.'"

(Quran 61:6)

According to this holy verse, Jesus gave tidings of a prophet to come after him named "Ahmad"(ṣ) which means highly praised. Furthermore, the companions of Prophet Muhammad (ṣ) are mentioned in the Torah (the Old Testament) and the gospel (the New Testament). But why aren't these references present in the current Torah and Gospel? The answer is that both the Torah and Gospel were distorted. Even though the content of the Old and New Testaments was tampered with, we may derive various references to Prophet Muhammad (ṣ) in them. Let's start with mention of Ishmael, Prophet Muhammad's (ṣ) ancestor:

In Genesis 17:20, God addresses Abraham as follows: "And as for Ishmael, I have heard you: I will surely bless him; I will make him fruitful and will greatly increase his numbers. He will be the father of twelve rulers, and I will make him into a great nation."

After nearly dying in the wilderness, Ishmael and his mother Hagar are saved by the Lord. God continues to be with Ishmael, blessing the boy as he grows into a man in a place called the wilderness of Paran. "'What troubles you, Hagar? Fear not; for God has heard the voice of the lad where he is. Arise, lift up the lad, and hold him fast with your hand; for I will make him a great nation.' Then God opened her eyes, and she saw a well of water; and she went, and filled the skin with water, and gave the lad a drink. And God was with the lad, and he grew up; he lived in the wilderness, and became an expert with the bow. He lived in the wilderness of Paran..." (Genesis 21:17-21)

Deuteronomy 33:1-2 mentions the land of Paran once again: "And he said, The Lord came from Sinai, and rose up from Seir unto them; he shined forth from mount Paran, and he came with ten thousand of saints: from his right hand went a fiery law for them." An interpretation of this verse may be as follows:

"Deuteronomy 33:1-2 combines references to Moses (peace be upon him), Jesus (peace be upon him) and Muhammad (blessings and peace be upon him). It speaks about God's revelation coming from Sinai, rising from Seir (probably the village of Sa'ir near Jerusalem) and shining forth from Paran. According to Genesis 21:21, the wilderness of Paran was the place where Ishmael (peace be upon him) settled (that is, in Arabia, specifically Makkah). Another sign of the prophet to come from Paran (Makkah) is that he will come with "ten thousand of saints" (Deuteronomy 33:2 KJV). That was the number of faithful who accompanied Prophet Muhammad (blessings and peace be upon him) to Makkah in his victorious, bloodless return to his birthplace to destroy the remaining symbols of idolatry in the Kaaba. The text says, "He shined forth from mount Paran, and he came with ten thousand of saints, from his right hand (went) a fiery law for them."[1]

Even though some exegetes have striven to identify Jesus as the one to exit from Mount Paran, there are two impediments to this explanation. There is no geographical connection which

---

1. Al-Rassi, Majed. The Amazing Prophecies of Muhammad in the Bible. 2013: p.40, 41.

links Jesus to Mount Paran, and Jesus did not come with a law but was a follower of Mosaic Law.[1] "God came from Teman, and the Holy One from the Mountain of Paran! The Heavens were covered from his brightness of splendor, and the Earth was filled with his praise!" (Habakkuk 3:3) This praise may be an indication of Prophet Muhammad (ṣ), as his name is derived from the Arabic word for praise and means "he who is greatly praised", and Mount Paran is the dwelling-place of his ancestor, Ishmael.

Furthermore, in the Gospel of John, Jesus mentions that God will send a "Paraclete" after him: "If you love me, you will keep my commandments. And I will ask the Father, and he will give you another Paraclete, that he may abide with you forever." (14:15-16)

What does "Paraclete" mean? John's Gospel explains its meaning as follows: "But the Paraclete, the Holy Spirit, whom the Father will send in my name, he will teach you all things, and bring to your remembrance all that I have said to you" (14:26), "he will bear witness to me" (15:26). The actions of the Paraclete are clarified as follows: "But when he, the Spirit of truth, comes, he will guide you into all the truth. He will not speak on his own; he will speak only what he hears, and he will tell you what is yet to come." (John 16:13)

Exegetes of the New Testament identify "Paraclete" with the Holy Spirit as you might have noticed from the previous text, but an alternative explanation may be presented. The French surgeon Maurice Bucaille writes how a single word in a passage from John concerning the Paraclete radically alters its meaning and completely changes its sense when viewed from a theological point of view: "The verb 'to hear', in the translation is the Greek verb 'akouô' meaning to perceive sounds. The verb 'to speak' in the translation is the Greek verb 'laleô' which has the general meaning of 'to emit sounds' and the specific

---

[1]. The Gospel of Matthew relates how Jesus said: "Do not think that I have come to abolish the Law or the Prophets. I have not come to abolish them, but to fulfill them." (Matthew 5:17)

meaning of 'to speak'. It therefore becomes clear that the communication to man which he here proclaims does not in any way consist of a statement inspired by the agency of the Holy Spirit. It has a very obvious material character moreover, which comes from the idea of the emission of sounds conveyed by the Greek word that defines it.

The two Greek verbs 'akouô' and 'laleô' therefore define concrete actions which can only be applied to a being with hearing and speech organs. It is consequently impossible to apply them to the Holy Spirit. If the words 'Holy Spirit' are omitted from the passage, the complete text of John then conveys a meaning which is perfectly clear. According to the rules of logic therefore, one is brought to see in John's Paraclete a human being like Jesus, possessing the faculties of hearing and speech formally implied in John's Greek text. Jesus therefore predicts that God will later send a human being to Earth to take up the role defined by John, i.e. to be a prophet who hears God's word and repeats his message to man. This is the logical interpretation of John's texts arrived at if one attributes to the words their proper meaning. The presence of the term 'Holy Spirit' in today's text could easily have come from a later addition made quite deliberately. It may have been intended to change the original meaning which predicted the advent of a prophet subsequent to Jesus and was therefore in contradiction with the teachings of the Christian churches at the time of their formation.[1] . Additionally, the phrase "but when he, the Spirit of truth, comes" indicates that this entity was not present during the time of Jesus while the gospels mention that the Holy Spirit descended a number of times upon Jesus and his disciples.

It is also worth noting that some versions do not contain the words "Holy Spirit" after the word Paraclete. The latter is derived from a Greek term Paraclytos which closely resembles the word Periclytos which means "praised one", which resembles the name of Prophet Muhammad (ṣ).

---

1. Bucaille, Maurice. The Bible, the Qur'an, and Science. P.79, 80.

B. Personal Attributes

A prophet's moral qualities facilitate belief in his message. People who have witnessed the honesty, integrity, wisdom and other commendable qualities of a messenger before the commencement of his mission readily believe his prophecy once he declares it. A person who has proven his monotheism, high ethical traits, and disdain for social standing and the vain display of wealth prior to his message will be more readily believed once he commences his mission.

A close examination of the details concerning the personality and conduct of a messenger, the holy book he brings forth, the content of his mission, and his companions provides numerous indications and signs regarding his truthfulness. When pieces of evidence accumulate, belief in the messenger is enforced, emphasizing the veracity of his claim.

Benefiting from signs and clues is applied in our everyday lives. For instance, a teacher can confirm that a middle school student has really written the elaborate poem he has just read in class by considering the rhythmic qualities and language used. If the poem displays signs of advanced authorship, it is safe to assume that someone older and wiser had composed the poem because a student who has still not studied advanced literary techniques would not be able to produce such a literary work.

We may apply this principle once we carefully consider the life of Prophet Muhammad (ṣ).[1] Prophet Muhammad (ṣ) was born in Mecca in the Arabian Peninsula, a geographical area with a harsh climate and overlooked by the great powers of that time. The inhabitants of the region were mostly uneducated and illiterate, and lacked access to Greek and Persian knowledge. They were mostly polytheistic despite the presence of some introversive Jewish communities which refrained from sharing Mosaic law with others. Idols were erected near the Sacred Mosque in Mecca and were revered by young and old, freemen and slaves. Arabs were fanatically attached to their tribes and

---

1. This inference was devised by Sayyed Muhammad Baqer al-Sadr.

at times engaged in bloody conflicts against each other. The individual derived his strength from his tribe, lineage and wealth. Additionally, they looked down upon women and some went as far as to bury their young daughters alive.

Prophet Muhammad (ṣ) lived among his tribe for forty years and was known for his lofty character long before the beginning of his mission. He was not in the least affected by the environment he lived in. He worshipped the One God and abhorred pagan idols. He was socially active and impressed people with his integrity and honesty. They placed their full trust in him upon witnessing his ethics, to the extent that he became known even before his prophethood as Al-Sadiq Al-Amin, the Truthful and Trustworthy One. Before embarking upon on a journey or a trade trip, many Arabs placed their cherished belongings in his care. He did not receive a formal, systematic education. He never sought authority or a rank of distinction nor did he espouse a certain branch of philosophy or an epistemic trend. He only traveled twice outside Mecca in a caravan. He was not acquainted with Judaism nor Christianity; if he had exerted an effort to learn about those two traditions, his people would have challenged his message.

Prophet Muhammad (ṣ) propagated his mission with full adherence to the holy verse:

"Invite to the way of your Lord with wisdom and good instruction, and argue with them in a way that is best. Indeed, your Lord is most knowing of who has strayed from His way, and He is most knowing of who is [rightly] guided."

(Quran 16:125)

Throughout thirteen years in Mecca and despite the suffering Prophet Muhammad (ṣ) endured, he did not resort to violence against the Meccans who inflicted harm upon him and his followers through various methods. As for the wars during the Medinan period, they were defensive in nature. Quraysh viewed the prophet's (ṣ) message as the greatest challenge, and strove to extinguish the spark of the new religion by waging wars against him. As for the Prophet's companions, they were not seekers of worldly interests. They intermingled together cordially, the young and the old, the rich and the poor, the socially distinguished and the sons of slaves.

From this brief introduction, we can contemplate the Religion of Truth. Islam represents a comprehensive message; it encompasses spiritual and material aspects, presents a mode of belief and conduct, and extends over cultural, economic and political domains. Islam is not an offshoot of any religion; it emphasizes values and presents a comprehensive and independent system of principles and dogmas, and governs all aspects of day-to-day life. It rectifies the distortions and deviations which had crept into previous monotheistic religions. It rejects all forms of polytheism and idolatry, and forbids unjust practices and dealings as usury.

Islam changed the criterion of preference which revolved around ancestry, tribal affiliation, or social status and introduced the criterion of piety. It championed the rights of women who had suffered severe forms of injustice during the pre-Islamic era, allowing them freedom of choice and opinion.

"O mankind, indeed We have created you from male and female and made you nations and tribes that you may know one another. Indeed, the most noble of you [in the sight of] Allah is the most pious of you. Indeed, Allah is Knowing, Aware."

(Quran 49:13)

As Bernard Lewis, a historian specialized in Oriental studies, puts it: "Islam has brought comfort and peace of mind to countless millions of men and women. It has given dignity and meaning to drab and impoverished lives. It has taught people of different races to live in brotherhood and people of different creeds to live side by side in reasonable tolerance. It inspired a great civilization in which others besides Muslims lived creative and useful lives and which, by its achievement, enriched the whole world."

C. Miracles

Miracles are extraordinary divine events that are not explicable by natural or scientific laws, and may not be contradicted or challenged by ordinary humans. God aided His prophets with miracles to prove their trustworthiness and connection with the divine. Once the connection is proven, the prophet's role as spiritual leader is established and the content of his message is authenticated.

Miracles are divine actions, performed by prophets by the will of God, and are not magic, illusions, or sleights of hand. They are beyond the bounds of ordinary humans. For instance, a person might undergo an operation to improve vision problems but science has still not found a cure for blindness. On the other hand, a prophet places his hand on a blind person's eyes and his sight is retrieved. The scientific prerequisites to conduct an eye operation may be learned and applied by any able person. On the other hand, miracles occur by divine permission and are not taught. Despite the fact that scientific advancement has reached new and previously inaccessible accomplishments, especially in medical matters, but miracles surpass imitation.

Due to the fact that miracles are inimitable, they are also unchallenged. When a prophet displays a divine miracle, he inevitably emerges triumphant since no contender will be able to produce a similar feat. Miracles prove the authenticity of the divine message of the prophet, and are not performed to prove personal strength or merit.

The Miracle of the Quran

Poetry retained a high status in the cultural heritage of the ancient Arabs. Orally transmitted poems reflected features of pre-Islamic Arabian society: intense tribal bigotry, polytheistic beliefs, and celebration of chivalry and personal strength. The Arabs' love for literary eloquence led them to compile the finest Arabic poetry, a collection of seven pre-Islamic Arabic odes, each considered to be its author's best piece. These were recorded on scrolls and hung on the walls of the Kaʿbah in

Mecca. In the markets of the Arabs, particularly the fair at the western Arabian town of ʿUkāẓ, competitions of poetry and musical performances were held periodically, attracting the most distinguished poet-musicians. Tribes boasted a main poet who accompanied the tribal chief at home and during his travels, and whose poetry served to spread news, militarily mobilize his clan, and praise, eulogize, or even lampoon a certain individual.

Taking this environment into account, and "given that the society of the Arabs revolved around this love of language, it naturally follows that the Prophet's miracle should be a literary masterpiece which exceeded the abilities of human power in terms of eloquence, style, understanding, and clarity of expression."[1]

The Quran challenged the pagans to produce a book similar to the Quran, but they were powerless to do so:

"Say: If mankind and the jinn gathered to produce the like of this Quran, they could not produce the like of it, even if they were to each other assistants."

(Quran 17:88)

Another challenge was to produce ten *surahs*:

"Or do they say, 'He invented it'? Say, 'Then bring ten surahs the like thereof, invented, and call [for assistance] upon whomever you can besides Allah, if you are truthful.'"

(Quran 11:13)

The Arab pagans who prided themselves on their eloquence and command of language were helpless and could not even produce a single surah:

"And if you are in doubt as to what We have sent down upon Our Servant [Muhammad], then produce a surah the like thereof and call upon your witnesses other than Allah, if you are truthful."

(Quran 2:23)

---

1. Ayad, Hussain. The Seal to what was Revealed: A Qur'anic Approach to Exegesis. Outskirts Press, Inc.: 2009, p.10.

The Holy Quran challenged the strong Arab literary tradition, calling upon Arabs to gather any distinguished literary figures they chose and to consult and aid one another in producing a single *surah* like the *surahs* of the Quran. Quraysh mobilized its resources, energy and regional influence to produce a single refutation of the Quran, but they sorely failed. Their lack of success led them to resort to Walid ibn al-Mughira, a man known for his eloquence, to refute the inimitability of the Quran, but when he heard it "he was struck into silence, his heart turned numb, his eloquence forsook him, his argument collapsed, his case was devastated, his impotence clearly appeared and his wits were befuddled." [1]

Upon hearing several verses, Walid ibn al-Mughira remarked: "What should I say about it? By God, there is no one among you who is more knowledgeable than me in poetry or who is more conversant than me in the *rajaz* meter of poetry or in the odes or the poetry composed by the jinn. By God, [the Quran] does not resemble any of this [that I know about]. There is a certain sweetness to his words, a certain grace. It demolishes what is inferior to it and it surely surpasses but cannot be surpassed."[2]

This challenge not only confounded the pagans of Mecca, but the adversaries of Islam as well until this very day. As the Quran is a holy book which transcends place and time, these verses are addressed to all disbelievers throughout the ages. It is important to stress that the miraculous aspect of the Quran is not only restricted to the eloquent use of language, but also encompasses various dimensions. Some have tried to imitate the Quran, but their attempts have turned out to be extremely weak in terms of language and expression, and are even humorous.

---

1. Vasalou, Sophia. "The Miraculous Eloquence of the Quran: General Trajectories and Individual Approaches". Journal of Qur'anic Studies. Edinburgh University Press: 2002, Volume 4, p.23.
2. The Seal to what was Revealed: A Qur'anic Approach to Exegesis, p.11.

There is a rhythm in Quranic verses which evokes human feelings. This rhythmical form also reflects the content conveyed –whether it is a compassionate verse calling upon humans to seek refuge in their creator, or a stern verse which admonishes the disbelievers. The Quran is able to express specific meanings and rich images by using sounds, achieving its intent without the need for musical instruments.

After failing to contradict the Quran, the Prophet's opponents from Quraysh strove to find another method to confront Islam. They resorted to Jewish scholars and asked them for questions on historical details unbeknownst to laymen in order to test Prophet Muhammad's (ṣ) knowledge. To their disappointment, Prophet Muhammad (ṣ) was able to provide answers to all of their questions despite the fact that he had received no formal education at the hands of an instructor, nor was he acquainted with the content of holy books, nor had he lived in a center of civilization and culture. Furthermore, Prophet Muhammad (ṣ) rectified the errors of the Jews.

"There was certainly in their stories a lesson for those of understanding. It is not a narration invented, but a confirmation of what was before it, and a detailed explanation of all things, and a guidance and a mercy for a people who believe."
(Quran 12:111)

The Jews possessed the Torah but it contained distortions, and this sparked disagreement among the Jews regarding their narratives. The verses of the Quran, however, exposed the truth.

"Indeed, this Quran narrates to the Children of Israel most of that over which they disagree."
(Quran 27:76)

"O People of the Scripture, there has come to you Our Messenger making clear to you much of what you used to conceal of the Scripture and overlooking much. There has come to you from Allah a light and a clear Book."
(Quran 5:15)

Thus, the people of Mecca could not oppose the historical accounts mentioned in the Quran.

"That is from the news of the unseen which We reveal to you, [O Muhammad]. You knew it not, neither you nor your people, before this. So be patient; indeed, the [best] outcome is for the pious."

(Quran 11:49)

Scientific Miracles in the Quran

It is important to state that the Holy Quran in its essence is a book which guides mankind and transports them from darkness into the light. It is not a chemistry, astrology, or physics book even though it contains numerous references to scientific findings.[1] These references are proof of the divine origin of the Quran as they were revealed more than 1400 years ago at a time when humans lacked knowledge of many cosmic and scientific facts which were only recently discovered and made accessible by technological advancement.

Throughout history, exegetes of the Quran have in their own capacity presented explanations to Quranic verses which include scientific references. But in the modern era, and with the emergence of new discoveries previously mentioned in the Quran, thousands have come to believe in this Holy Book which hundreds of years ago mentioned scientific facts only discovered recently. It is worth noting that these verses serve as a guidance to mankind, to open their eyes to the signs of God; if it weren't for this purpose, scientific references would not have been mentioned in the Quran.

---

1. Islam encourages the pursuit of scientific knowledge; for instance: solving mathematical equations, performing laboratory experiments, and achieving scientific discoveries which serve the interest of society. At the same time, Islam condemns the usage of science and technology to exercise hegemony and subjugation.

In what follows are a few examples of these references

Geology:

A Quranic verse mentions that mountains are "bulwarks" or "pegs" (Quran 78:6), while another verse explains their function:

"And He has cast into the earth firmly set mountains, lest it shift with you, and [made] rivers and roads, that you may be guided."
(Quran 16:15)

A peg is an object used to pin down or fasten things, such as a tent. It has been discovered that the majority part of a mountain extends underground as a root as far as 10-15 times its actual height on the surface of the Earth. The formation of a mountain arises from the collision of two massive tectonic plates where the stronger plate slides under the other and makes a deep extension while the weaker one bends and forms the mountain on the surface. The mountain acts as earth's crust stabilizer, and this process is known as isostasy. Isostasy is the general equilibrium in the Earth's crust maintained by a yielding flow of rock material beneath the surface under gravitational stress.[1]

Motion of the Wind:

The Quran mentions how the wind fulfills the following function.

"And We have sent the winds fertilizing, and sent down water from the sky, then given it to you to drink. And you are not its retainers."
(Quran 15:22)

According to an interpretation, this verse refers to the natural process of wind pollination which ensures the propagation of various plant species. "Whether it's a blowing winter gale or a soft summer breeze, the wind has an effect on the ecology of

---

[1]. Ibrahim, Mohammad Akhiruddin. "Mountains as Stabilizers of the Earth from A Quranic Perspective", p.1232-1233.

plants and animals. Wind has the ability to help things move, that otherwise couldn't, around their environment. Seeds are one of the most common things that are moved by the wind…Other plants use the wind to create seeds. Many trees, especially pine and oak trees, use the wind to disperse pollen with the hope that the pollen will travel to and fertilize a viable egg where, under the right conditions, a seed will develop. Insects may help the process, but if you have ever lived in an area dominated by pine and oak trees, you've seen the generous amounts of pollen released by the male structures. It's a natural mechanism to ensure that the genetic material in the pollen will fertilize as many eggs as possible, thereby passing on the legacy of the tree."[1]

Many of the world's most important crop plants are wind-pollinated. These include wheat, rice, corn, rye, barley and oats. Many economically important trees are also wind-pollinated. These include pines, spruces, firs and many hardwood trees, including several species cultivated for nut production .[2]

Another interpretation of this verse points to the role the wind plays in the formation of raindrops in clouds. Researchers still have difficulty explaining why raindrops form. New research shows that wind turbulence can play a crucial role. Swirling winds inside clouds may be one of the keys to the quick formation of raindrops. Inside clouds tiny vortices created by the wind spin water-sodden dust particles into clusters, where they meld to form raindrops. This discovery may eventually help meteorologists predict storms with better accuracy.[3]

---

1. Crick, Julie. "Wind is Essential to Natural Processes". Michigan State University Extension. March 30, 2017.

2. Weiseman, Wayne; Halsey, Daniel; Ruddock, Bryce. Integrated Forest Gardening. Chelsea Green Publishing: 2014, p.179.

3. Brumfiel, Geoff. "How Raindrops Form". Phys.Rev.Focus. March 22, 2001.

Origin of the Universe:

"Have those who disbelieve not considered that the heavens and the earth were a joined entity, then We separated them and made from water every living thing? Will they not then believe?"

(Quran 21:30)

This verse states that the heavens and the earth in their initial state were merged together, but were separated in a certain moment. This may be explained by the Big Bang theory which was introduced in 1964 and holds that the rapid expansion of matter from a state of extremely high density and temperature marked the origin of the universe. According to the theory, the universe as we know it started 13.8 billion years ago with an infinitely hot, infinitely dense singularity, then inflated -first at unimaginable speed, and then at a more measurable rate -to the cosmos that we know today.

The Quran states that every living thing is made of water. The World Water Council gives this description of the importance of water: "Water is life. All living organisms are predominantly made of water: human beings about 60%, fish about 80%, plants between 80% and 90%. Water is necessary for all chemical reactions that occur in living cells-(it) is essential for food production and all living ecosystems."[1]

Expansion of the Universe:

"And the Firmament We constructed with strength, and indeed, We are [its] expander."

(Quran 51:47)

Modern science has discovered the expansion of the universe: "The galaxies outside of our own are moving away from us, and the ones that are farthest away are moving the fastest. This means that no matter what galaxy you happen to be in, all the other galaxies are moving away from you. However, the galaxies are not moving through space, they are moving in space, because space is also moving. In other words, the

---

1. Science Education Resource Center at Carleton College, website.

universe has no center; everything is moving away from everything else… One famous analogy to explain the expanding universe is imagining the universe like a loaf of raisin bread dough. As the bread rises and expands, the raisins move farther away from each other, but they are still stuck in the dough. In the case of the universe, there may be raisins out there that we can't see any more because they have moved away so fast that their light has never reached Earth."[1]

There are many other examples from various scientific domains, and whoever would like to study the scientific miracles in the Quran may refer to independent books on this topic.

---

1. Library of Congress, website. Question: What does it mean when they say the universe is expanding?

CHAPTER FIVE
MAN AS VICEGERENT

THE HOLY QURAN provides humans with essential knowledge and guides them to the purpose of their existence and their expected role. Independent reasoning fails to aid us in reaching answers to our existential concerns, and this makes us in constant need of revelation.

A comprehensive study of the Quran aids us in comprehending divine actions. Once the wisdom behind divine actions is revealed, one may grasp fundamental concepts stated in the Quran such as the conflict between Truth and Falsehood, the significance of the *Sharia*, and the role of ethics in human life. An extensive study of the Quranic text reveals a comprehensive system of laws and ethical guidelines. All of this leads us to understand that God's actions are characterized by meaning and are not frivolous nor vain.

The Quran describes divine actions in two ways: they are free of frivolity and they are characterized by the *truth*. The following verses awaken humans to the fact that God's actions are not aimless, and that life pulsates with meaning.

- *"Did you then think that We created you uselessly and that to Us you would not be returned?"*

(Quran 23:115)

- *"And We did not create the heavens and earth and what is between them in play."*

(Quran 44:38)

Furthermore, believers should not keep company with those who seek the satisfaction of worldly pleasures and the attainment of material gains, and who display no concern toward the afterlife. This carelessness toward the eternal life is a reason why such individuals should be avoided.

- *"So turn away from whoever turns [his back] on Our remembrance and desires nothing but the worldly life.*

That is their sum of knowledge. Indeed, your Lord is most knowing of who strays from His way, and He is most knowing of who is guided."

(Quran 53:29-30)

-*"And leave those who take their religion as play and diversion and whom the worldly life has deluded."*

(Quran 6:70)

Two descriptions are given in aforementioned holy verse: la'eb and *lahw*, translated as play and diversion respectively. *La'eb* is the involvement in play while *lahw* may be explained as an engagement in a less important action and forsaking a more important one, therefore contradicting wisdom since a wise person is expected to fulfill his/her actions in order of priority.

The Quran states that an individual who neglects the connection between the worldly life and the hereafter only possesses shallow knowledge.

"They know an outward [part] of the worldly life, but they, of the Hereafter, are heedless."

(Quran 30:7)

The worldly life is an arena of amusement and diversion if one refrains from paying heed to the afterlife and suffices himself with this temporal existence. When you realize that there is an eternal life awaiting you, and that faith and righteous deeds in this world have the greatest impact on your eternal fate, your worldly life becomes a means to attain never-ending bliss. Every second on earth gains special significance because the eternal reward relies upon the actions you are performing here and now. The hereafter is the true life which you should aspire to.

"And this worldly life is nothing but diversion and play. And indeed, the home of the Hereafter -that is the Life, if only they knew."

(Quran 29:64)

The Quran mentions those who use their intellectual faculties to contemplate the beauty and design in the heavens and the earth. They see the world for what it is and are not blinded by its attractions, and they reach the conclusion that the wonders which they behold have not been created in vain but are the handiwork of a Wise Creator who placed us on earth for a reason.

"Truly in the creation of the heavens and the earth and the alteration of the night and the day are signs for the possessors of intellect,

Who remember God standing, sitting, and lying on their sides, and reflect upon the creation of the heavens and the earth, 'Our Lord, You have not created this in vain. Glory be to You; then protect us from the torment of the Fire.'"

(Quran 3:190-191)

Truth Permeates Existence

"The Qur'an contains statements that indicate purpose and wisdom in God's act of creating everything in the best way (Q 32:7). Similarly, God creates with truth *(bil-haqq)* (Q 64:3), which can be interpreted as creation being molded according to a just and meaningful purpose. Similarly, God has not created the world in vain *(batila)* (Q 38:27). Based on such passages, theologians of various schools agree on God being infinitely wise. They all deny the possibility of injustice or absurdity in divine actions."[1]

The Quran mentions that God created the heavens and earth "in truth", and this may be an indication "that the world is created with precision and perfection, and that the nature of the created world is just".[2]

*-"We did not create the heavens and earth and what is between them except **in truth** and [for] a specified term. But those who disbelieve, from that of which they are warned, turn away."*

(Quran 46:3)

---

1. The Oxford Handbook of Wisdom and the Bible, p.234.

2. The Study Quran, p.2253.

-*"Do they not contemplate within themselves? Allah has not created the heavens and the earth and what is between them except **in truth** and for a specified term. And indeed, many among mankind, are disbelievers in the meeting with their Lord."*

(Quran 30:8)

Another verse describes how angels descend "in truth":

*"We do not send down the angels except **in truth** and (the disbelievers) would not then be reprieved."*

(Quran 15:8)

"Truth" has various meanings, but when discussing divine aims it indicates an action which suits the performer[1]. He who is wise performs actions which serve a purpose, and his characteristics are reflected in his actions. Therefore, everything you witness around you, from a buzzing hummingbird to dandelions drifting on the wind, from snow-capped mountains to the sand dunes of the desert, all exist for a reason.

The Quran guides us to various reasons behind the creation of humans, and these may be presented as follows:

TRIALS AND TRIBULATIONS

The Quran links creation with the divine test of mankind. God created humans and placed them on a unique planet with ideal factors permitting life, so that man –the *khalifa*- can be tried and tested, attaining perfection through his own will. This world is a testing ground, an experimental station, where one chooses between faith and disbelief, virtue or vice, and morality or depravity.

"And it is He who created the heavens and the earth in six days -and His Throne was upon water- that He might test you as to which of you is best in conduct."

(Quran 11:7)

---

1. Mesbah Yazdi, Taqi. Ma'aref al-Quran, p.221.

Another verse mentions how the ornaments of Earth, our temporary home, are a test for mankind.

"Indeed, We have made that which is on the earth adornment for it that We may test them [as to] which of them is best in conduct. And surely We shall make whatsoever is upon it a barren plain!"

(Quran 18:7-8)

All of the beauty you see on earth shall turn into a barren plain, and none of its adornments will endure forever, but will come to end and return to God[1]. Generations of mankind have lived -or are yet to be born- on earth. Some will be entranced by earthly adornments and forget the afterlife, while others will not be deceived and shall see the worldly life for what it is: a temporal existence on a planet which will be transformed into a barren plain. Close your eyes and imagine the future of earth, no vegetation, forests, or water. All of its material attractions will turn to waste. This is not your real home, why satisfy yourself with a perishable place you were not meant for?

The adornments of Earth are not the only factors which serve as a test for mankind. The following verse clarifies that life and death meet this aim as well.

"[He] who created death and life that He may try you as to which of you is most virtuous in deed; and He is the Mighty, the Forgiving."

(Quran 67:2)

This verse suggests that "trials are an inherent part of the human condition. The trials one encounters in life are not unjust, for God tasks no soul beyond its capacity, but rather are a necessary part of one's journey in this life; when met with the correct response, they can only help strengthen one spiritually, improve one's character, and increase one's love for God and trust in Him. From this perspective, trials are a blessing and a mercy from God." [2]

---

1. The Study Quran, p.1333
2. The Study Quran, p.1037.

God tests humans with both good and evil, fortune and misfortune. How individuals act in times of bliss or during times of hardship specifies if they have passed the test or not.

"Every soul shall taste death. And We test you with evil and with good, as a trial; and to Us shall you be returned."

(Quran 21:35)

It is important to remember that "both evil and good can be trials as in 7:168: *'And We tried them with good things and with evil things'*; that is, one can be tried with sickness as well as good health, poverty as well as wealth, error as well as guidance. Or people are tried as to whether they will do what is obligatory and abstain from what is forbidden. The test by what is good is whether one will be grateful to God and be generous with what God provides, and the test by what is evil is whether one will be patient."[1]

Contrary to what some people may believe, trials are not only restricted to hardship or instances of suffering such as sickness, lack of sustenance, war, or loss of loved ones. God also tests humans with endowments and favorable conditions such as the possession of wealth, fame, intelligence, and beauty. It is up to us to pass the divine test. Will we exhibit patience in times of hardship, or gratitude in times of fortune? It is worth noting how the Quran combines between these two traits -patience and gratitude- in various verses. [2]

*"Indeed in that are signs for every **patient** [and] **grateful** one."*

(Quran 14:5)

Patience is not merely a passive state where an individual remains silent and refrains from complaining. Patience is a vibrant choice, marked by perseverance in the face of problems and endurance during adversity. It is a continuous struggle to never give up. Likewise, gratitude does not only mean saying "thank you God". It involves making use of divine grants and

---

1. Ibid., p.1485.
2. Refer to Quran: 14:5; 34:19; 13:5; 31:31.

favors to perform virtuous deeds[1]. In all forms of divine tests, you need firm willpower to succeed.

Explaining Divine Tests

The purpose of divine tests is not the discovery of the quality of humans, because God is fully aware of each and every human being. Divine trials are not compared to academic tests where the level of performance reveals the amount of knowledge a person possesses. God tests His servants so that their merit may be revealed and their inner beauty may be uncovered. When you pass the divine test, your moral excellence, personal strength and resilience may shine through. "Life on earth is just the dress rehearsal before the real production. You will spend far more time on the other side of death-in eternity-than you will here. Earth is the staging area, the preschool, the tryout for your life in eternity… This life is preparation for the next. At most, you will live a hundred years on earth, but you will spend forever in eternity."[2]

Consider the following example. Military training is a physically and psychologically intensive process. Personnel are trained at a military camp where they are deprived of food, shelter, and sleep and where they learn to cope with harsh conditions. The combination of intense physical training and field exercises makes individuals strong and capable. It is a tough process, but a rewarding one. Once training is complete, the recruit will have sharpened his concentration, endurance and resolution. Without this training period and the determination to endure mental and physical exhaustion, these capabilities would not have been strengthened.

In life, you can choose between the Straight Path or moral deviation, offering righteous deeds or committing sins. This

---

1. An attractive outer appearance should not be exploited to arouse sinful lusts, charity should be paid from one's wealth, physical prowess and technological strength should be used to aid others and not to oppress the weak.
2. Warren, Rick. The Purpose-Driven Life. Zondervan: 2002: p.36.

may be further clarified by a passage from *Nahj al-Balagha* where Imam Ali (8) states the following:

> "None of you should say, 'O Allah! I seek Your protection from affliction' because there is none who is not [afflicted]. But whoever seeks [Allah's] protection should seek it from misguiding troubles because Allah, the Glorified, says: *'And know that your wealth and your children are a trial'* (Quran, 8:28). It means that He, the Glorified, tries His servants with wealth and progeny in order to distinguish one who is displeased with his livelihood from one who is satisfied with what he has been allotted. Even though [Allah], the Glorified, knows them more than they know themselves, but in order for actions to appear by which the reward or punishment is deserved." [1]

Humans have the ability to perform good or evil, to adopt positive qualities or display negative ones. You can be patient or temperamental, courageous or cowardly, considerate or rude. The reward or chastisement depends on the course of action you have willingly decided to take and how you reflect your inner capacities. You are honest when you exhibit upright principles and refrain from lying, and you are loyal when you choose to be faithful to your commitments rather than resorting to betrayal and treachery.

The Quran mentions two prophets who went through different circumstances. The first one, Solomon, was a prophet-ruler of a magnificent kingdom and a possessor of extensive wealth and power, while the second one, Job, was a prophet who suffered from sickness and the loss of cherished family members. Both were tested, and both succeeded. It is striking that these two figures are given a special designation in the Quran *"ni'm al-'abd"* which may be translated as *"excellent servant"*.

- *"And to David We gave Solomon. An excellent servant, indeed he was one repeatedly turning back [to Allah]."*

---

1. Some parts of the translation have been derived from: Peak of Eloquence, edited by Yasin T. Al-Jibouri. Tahrike Tarsile Qur'an, Inc, p.848.

(Quran 38:30)

-*"Indeed, We found him [Job] patient. An excellent servant. Indeed, he was one repeatedly turning back [to Allah]."*

(Quran 38:44)

Job was patient despite his emotional suffering and physical ailment, while Solomon was not blinded by the profuseness of wealth and power which God had granted him. We can also notice how Solomon was aware that the bliss he enjoyed was a divine test, evident through the following verse:

"This is from the favor of my Lord to test me whether I will be grateful or ungrateful."

(Quran 27:40)

Furthermore, Solomon responds to the divine order, *"Work, O family of David, in gratitude"* (Quran 34:13), and asks God to aid him in offering thankfulness (and therefore passing the divine test):

"My Lord, enable me to be thankful for Your favor which You have bestowed upon me and upon my parents and to do righteousness of which You approve."

(Quran 27:19)

Divine Tests and Diversity

Diversity among humans is a source of beauty, whether in terms of skin color, skills, language, prowess and outer appearance. If humans were all alike in mental and physical characteristics, life would lack richness and vibrancy. Just like an abundancy in gold would make it lose its value, so would a world filled with humans who possess the same interests and talents make earth a dull place. There is a beauty in the diversity among the billions of people who call this planet home; in their unique facial features, fingerprints, voices, and modes of expression. The Quran draws attention to this beauty in diversity:

> *"And of His signs is the creation of the heavens and the earth and the difference in your languages and colors. Indeed, in that are signs for those who know."*
>
> (Quran 30:22)

Reference is also made to the differences in divine endowments granted to humans:

> *"Do they distribute the mercy of your Lord? We have apportioned among them their livelihood in the life of [this] world and have raised some of them above others in ranks that they may take one another for service. And the mercy of your Lord is better than that which they accumulate."*
>
> (Quran 43:32)

No matter how hard you try to count your blessings, you can never make a full estimate of the endowments God has granted you. Health, intelligence, a loving family, a sound memory, talent, and security are just a few. Let's take the following table into consideration where a hypothetical rating out of 10 is allotted to every blessing for every person. This draws attention to the fact that there is a difference in the distribution of blessings, but every person has something which the other may lack.

Individual \ Blessing	Wealth	Beauty	Intelligence	Strength	Security
A	8	2	5	1	9
B	1	9	4	2	8
C	4	1	9	2	5
D	5	2	8	9	4

Difference in distribution reflects divine wisdom, and no one is entirely lacking in blessings. From here, it is important to clarify two points:

a- You might cherish a certain blessing more than others, but the loss of any blessing will lead you to rue its absence and awaken you to its significance. This is why, for instance, wealth becomes insignificant if a person is afflicted with disease or is stranded in a war-torn country.

b- One might deem it "unfair" and "unlucky" that he lacks a certain blessing or doesn't have enough of it. But always keep in mind that the distribution of graces conforms to divine wisdom. It is important to remember that the future might hold pleasant surprises in store. What you wish for today may be yours tomorrow. And if you don't attain that which you desire, you should keep in mind that there is a divine wisdom in that. You will be asked in the afterlife how you benefited from divine bestowals, and you will be recompensed for what you have lost.

> *"Do not grieve over past joys, be sure*
> *They will reappear in another form.*
> *A child's joy is in milk and nursing*
> *but once weaned, it finds new joy*
> *in bread and honey.*
> *Joy appears in many different forms*
> *it moves from place to place.*
> *It may suddenly show in the falling rain*
> *or in the rose bed; it comes now as water,*
> *now as beauty, or as nourishing bread.*
> *But suddenly it may show its face*
> *from behind the veil and destroy all idols*
> *that prevent you from seeking the Divine."* [1]
> -Rumi

When it comes to blessings, it is important to focus on two states of mind: contentment and aspiration. You should be

---

1. Rumi's Little Book of Life, p.4.

pleased with what God has given you because He distributes grants according to His wisdom. True joy should be in the mercy of God, and not in perishable worldly possessions: *"And the mercy of your Lord is better than whatever they accumulate."*

Don't remain in a passive state. It is true that there are things which you can't alter, but whenever there is room for change to the better, rouse yourself and take action.

"Indeed, Allah alters not what is in a people until they alter what is in themselves."

(Quran 13:11)

God tests us with diversity: In poverty, will you be patient? In wealth, humble and grateful? Will you be merciful toward fellow humans if you possess power? Will you be modest despite your attractive outer appearance?

SERVITUDE

The Quran clearly states that servitude to God is the purpose behind the creation of free, rational beings.

"And I did not create the jinn and mankind except to worship Me."

(Quran 51:56)

Servitude to God is a personal decision. It is your choice. The Quran mentions how the pagans falsely cast responsibility for their idolatry unto God:

"Those who associated [partners with Allah] will say: If Allah had willed, we would not have associated [partners to Him] and neither would our fathers, nor would we have prohibited anything."

(Quran 6:148)

Humans have the choice between servitude or disbelief. Even though every true believer wishes that all humans on earth would embrace faith, God clarifies that belief is a choice and is not enforced upon anyone. God is fully able to turn all human beings into believers, but has given them the choice to willingly choose their course of life. Many humans simply refuse to believe, and forcing them to have faith would only strip their belief of value.

-"Do not those who believe know that, had Allah willed, He could have guided all mankind?"

(Quran 13:31)

-"And had your Lord willed, those on earth would have believed, all of them entirely. Then would you compel mankind until they become believers?"

(Quran 10:99)

Actions performed under compulsion lack significance because they are not performed freely, sincerely, or wholeheartedly. If an individual were forced to emulate divine attributes and be compassionate, generous and wise, could s/he be described as an individual seeking perfection? Suppose someone forces another to give money to an orphanage. This apparent act of kindness would not deserve praise because if left to his own choice, that person would have refrained from donating. On the other hand, voluntary acts of compassion are met with appreciation and praise.

Servitude to God is the purpose of creation, but God does not force humans to express their devotion. Man is divinely guided and granted the means to advance on the path of servitude, but with his own choice.

"Indeed, We created man from a sperm-drop mixture [that] We [may] try him; and We made him hearing [and] seeing. Indeed, We guided him to the way, be he grateful or ungrateful."

(Quran 76:2-3)

To reach perfection, there are two important factors. The first is following divine guidance, encouraged by the fitra which can never be eradicated (though it might become veiled), aided by the intellect, and inspired by revelation.

"Indeed, [incumbent] upon Us is guidance."

(Quran 92:12)

"Glorify the name of your Lord, the Most High, Who created, then proportioned. And who measured, then guided."

(Quran 87: 1-3)

You will face obstacles on the way and impediments to stop you from advancing. On every corner there will be a lurking demon, an enticing temptation, or a worldly attraction. But if you have a sincere heart, God will protect you from falling prey to the traps which await you.

"And those who strive for Us, We will surely guide them to Our ways. And indeed, Allah is with the doers of good."

(Quran 29:69)

The second factor is human determination. God shows you the way and aids you in traversing it, but responsibility for the choice you take lies upon your own shoulders. This "way" involves the "purification of the soul". The human spirit requires self-rectification in order to transcend and gain perfection.

"And [by] the soul and He who proportioned it, Then inspired it [with discernment of] its wickedness and its righteousness, He has succeeded who purifies it, And he has failed who obscures it."

(Quran 91:7-10)

These last two verses "have served as the inspiration for extensive literature on the 'purification of the soul', which some argue is the entire purpose of the Quran... The text speaks of those who cleanse the soul of lowly and despicable character traits and, conversely, those who dull the soul by neglecting it through heedlessness and disobedience. According to some of the earliest commentators, these two verses could also be read with God as the subject, meaning, 'He whose soul God purifies has indeed prospered, and he whose soul God obscures has indeed failed'."[1]

---

1 The Study Quran, p.2772.

The ambiguity of the subject can also be considered as an allusion to how purification is done through God and human beings "who work together to purify the soul, for, on the one hand, *'Whosoever purifies himself purifies himself only for his own soul'* (35:18), and on the other, *'You do not will but that God wills'* (76:30); thus 4:49 states, *'Rather, it is God Who purifies whomsoever He will'*. Nonetheless, there is a subtle reciprocity in every step one takes toward God, for as 13:11 proclaims: *Truly God alters not what is in a people until they alter what is in themselves.*"[1]

DIVINE MERCY

Divine wisdom and mercy are reflected in all creatures, but there is a special mercy which is bestowed upon man, the *khalifa* of God, who voluntarily strives toward perfection by sincere worship and emulates divine attributes. The origin of creation is mercy, and the sublime, final aim is mercy.

> *"And if your Lord had willed, He could have made mankind one community; and they will not cease to differ.*
> *Except those upon whom your Lord has mercy, and for that He created them..."*
> (Quran 11:118-119)

God bestowed his mercy unconditionally upon humans when He created them, but divine mercy which God grants to humans in the hereafter is a reward for fortitude during trials and reverent love and honor paid to God through conscious worship. The ultimate aim of creation is for divine mercy to encompass humans, and this is evident through the dispatch of Prophet Muhammad (ṣ) as a messenger:

> *"And We have not sent you, [O Muhammad], except as a mercy to the worlds."*
> (Quran 21:107)

---

1 Ibid, p.2772.

Therefore, when an individual chooses to be a sincere follower of Prophet Muhammad (ṣ) and strives toward high moral characteristics and virtuous deeds, divine mercy awaits.

-"Say, [O Muhammad, to mankind]: If you love Allah, then follow me; Allah will love you and forgive you your sins. And Allah is Forgiving, Merciful."

(Quran 3:31)

-"So those who believe in Allah and hold fast to Him -He will admit them to mercy from Himself and bounty and guide them to Himself [upon] a straight path."

(Quran 4:175)

-"And as for those whose faces [will] turn white, [they will be] in the mercy of Allah, therein dwelling forever."

(Quran 3:107)

Conversely, many humans have obscured the light of *fitra*, rejecting belief, committing sins and deviating from the Straight Path.

-"And the ones who disbelieve in the signs of Allah and the meeting with Him- those have despaired of My mercy, and those will have a painful torment."

(Quran 29:23)

-"Yes, whoever earns evil and his sin has encompassed him -those are the companions of the Fire; they will abide therein eternally."

(Quran 2:81)

The Quran contains several references to the divine mercy bestowed upon the prophets.

God teaches his beloved prophet Muhammad (ṣ), and ourselves, the following supplication:

"And say, 'My Lord, forgive and have mercy, and You are the best of the merciful.'"

(Quran 23:118)

God mentions the mercy which he bestowed upon the prophets, naming several of them whom He admitted into His mercy such as Ismail, Idris, Thul-Kifl and Lot (in another verse).

"And We admitted them into Our mercy. Indeed, they are among the righteous."

(Quran 21:86)

Moses beseeches God, requesting admittance into divine mercy for himself and his brother Aaron:

"He said, 'My Lord, forgive me and my brother and admit us into Your mercy, and You are the most merciful of the merciful.'"

(Quran 7:151)

God created you through His mercy.

He manages your affairs and extricates you from harm's way through His mercy.

He alleviates your pain and saves you from distress by His mercy.

He supports you, even during the tests to which He has subjected you, by His mercy.

Mercy surrounds you from all sides, gentle, abounding, and empowering, but there is still a special mercy which you should aspire for, one that awaits you in the hereafter. The course of human life may be summarized as follows: Humans were created to be tested, to offer willing servitude to God, and to be encompassed in eternal mercy.

HUMAN VICEGERENCY

This discussion on the purpose of creation according to the Holy Quran can never be complete without reference to human vicegerency on Earth. This will take us to the first days of humanity, to the story of Adam as the Quran relates it. Despite the diversity in creatures, God in His wisdom specifically chose man to be a *khalifa*, a vicegerent.

"And when your Lord said to the angels, 'Indeed, I am placing upon the earth a vicegerent.' They said, 'Will You place upon it one who causes corruption therein and sheds blood, while we declare Your praise and sanctify You?' Allah said, 'Indeed, I know that which you do not know.'"

(Quran 2:30)

"Vicegerent renders *khalīfah*, a word that can also mean 'successor' or 'deputy,' hence *khalīfat rasūl Allāh*, or "successor/steward of God's Messenger," shortened to *khalīfah* (anglicized as "caliph"). In some verses, such as here and 6:165, *khalīfah* appears to denote a universal human inheritance and responsibility, since all human beings are in their inner reality the *khalīfah* of God. In others, the sense of 'successor' comes to the fore."[1]

The question the angels posed did not arise from malice or envy toward Adam, but from puzzlement at the placement of a *khalifa* who would shed blood and spread corruption on earth. This was not an objection on their part, but an expression of wonder rather than doubt. How could this creature - molded from clay, granted mental and physical power, misled by lusts and desires, and given the choice between good and evil- serve a sublime purpose? But God had a special plan for this human being whom He had granted special knowledge.

"And He taught Adam the names, all of them. Then He presented them to the angels and said, 'Tell me the names of these, if you are truthful.'"

(Quran 2:31)

It soon became clear that Adam possessed a qualification which justified the importance God had attributed to him: knowledge of the Names. What is meant by the Names is not specified in the Quran and is a matter of interpretation.

---

1. Ibid., p.108.

*"Do thou hear the name of every thing from the Knower: hear the meaning of the mystery of **He taught Adam the Names.***

With us, the name of every thing is its outward form; with the Creator, its inward essence."[1]

-Rumi

According to gnostic thinkers in the Muslim tradition, the "names taught by God to humankind are none other than the 'beautiful names' of God himself. In imparting knowledge of His names, not only does God teach human beings to recognize all of the divine attributes of perfection, but He also gives them the ability to display those attributes consciously and, in so doing, act as God's representative on earth…It is on account of people's potential to act as God's representative that the angels were asked to acknowledge humankind's creational status by bowing down to them. In the cosmology of the Qur'an, angels are endowed with limited knowledge of God's names, and while they worship God with perfect sincerity and awareness, they do so because they lack the free will to disobey. Humans, on the other hand, are endowed not only with knowledge of all of God's names, but also with free will: if human beings use their knowledge of the names wisely and bow down to God of their own volition, they rise above the angels and fulfill their destiny as the jewel in the crown of creation. However, if they abuse their knowledge of the names and fail to fulfil their part of the 'trust', they sink to a position described by the Quran as the 'lowest of the low'."[2]

He who remains steadfast despite all the allurements of the worldly life and Satan's tricks is more elevated in rank than the angels who glorify God out of their nature. This is why individuals such as Muhammad (ṣ), Noah, Abraham, Moses and Jesus reached positions higher than angels.

Another interpretation states that the Names refer to certain spiritually-noble descendants of Adam: "We know this from the use of the pronoun hum meaning 'their' in the compound

---

1. Nicholson, Reynold. Selected Poems of Rumi. Dover Publications: 2011, p. 40.
2. Turner, Colin. Islam: The Basics. Routledge: 2006, p.191.

'their names' –which is used for conscious beings. It shows that Adam's descendants are included among the 'names' taught to him...The angels must have fully comprehended Adam's supremacy and the wisdom in his vicegerency, not merely because of his being taught the names that they had not been taught, but also because they saw the illustrious members of humankind among the descendants of Adam – such as the Prophets, saints, and pure, exacting scholars, who would change the earth into gardens of Paradise through their faith, knowledge, and morality." [1]

Adam was then instructed to reveal his knowledge. Upon discovering the potential of the human race, the angels declared:

"They said, 'Exalted are You; we have no knowledge except what You have taught us. Indeed, it is You who is the Knowing, the Wise.'"

(Quran 2:32)

Therefore, it became clear that man, formed of a spiritual composite –the divine breath- and a material composite, bore an essence which made him worthy of the reverence of the angels.

-*"And [mention] when We said to the angels, 'Prostrate before Adam'; so they prostrated, except for Iblis. He refused and was arrogant and was of the disbelievers."*

(Quran 2:34)

-*"So, when I have proportioned him and breathed into him of My Spirit, then fall down, prostrating yourselves to him."*

(Quran 15:29)

-*"Indeed, We created you, then We formed you, then We said to the angels, 'Prostrate yourselves to Adam.' So they all prostrated, except Iblis; he was not among those who prostrated."*

(Quran 7:11)

---

1 The Qur'an with Annotated Interpretation in Modern English, p.27

"We created you, then We formed you is addressed to all human beings, who are considered to have been originally created along with Adam as the seed in his loins. As such, all human beings can be understood as having participated in the events of the narrative that follows and in the nobility God bestows upon Adam, and are thus subject to the commands and the warnings issued to him."[1]

Khilāfa does not involve forcing humans to abide by the requirements and regulations of vicegerency. It rather means that the Lord of the heavens and earth has assigned mankind to control the earth and work on its social and natural development.[2] "As a term, khilāfah or vicegerency denotes improving the earth, on the basis of knowledge of things and the laws of creation (which we wrongly call the 'laws of nature'), and ruling on the earth according to the dictates of God, thus establishing justice"[3]. God did not leave humans in the world without a guide to face Satan's whispers, battle temptations, and control impulses on their own. Without divine intervention, man would not be able to fulfill the grand aims which God has placed for him.[4] This is stated clearly in God's address to Adam and Eve after falling from divine grace:

"We said, 'Get down from it, all of you. So when guidance comes to you from Me, whosoever follows My guidance, no fear shall be upon them, nor shall they grieve.'"

(Quran 2:38)

We may derive the following points from the account of creation:

1-The greatest priority in human life should be the connection with God, the creator and appointer of man as vicegerent. From Him is the origin, and to Him is the return.

---

1. Ibid., p.761.
2. Sadr, Mohammad Baqer. Islam Leads Life.
3. Ünal, Ali. The Qur'an with Annotated Interpretation in Modern English. Tughra Books: 2008, p.27.
4. Ibid.

Monotheism is the means of eternal salvation and the highest principle from which all other values spring forth.

2-Vicegerency does not imply that humans have been granted unchecked power or are allowed to act as they please. Humans are responsible for the earth and are expected to act wisely, spreading truth and justice and implementing reform on the individual and social level. This endeavor bears fruit in the world and the hereafter.

"Whoever does righteousness, whether male or female, and he is a believer -We will surely cause him to live a good life, and We will surely give them their reward [in the Hereafter] according to the best of what they used to do."

(Quran 16:97)

Humans' "happiness, dignity, and the improvement of the earth lie in acknowledging their innate weakness, poverty, and ignorance before God and, attributing whatever they have and their accomplishments to God."[1]

3-Man may become a *khalifa* by free will, implementing the *khilafa* on earth and collectively emulating the just and divinely-inspired ruling systems of Prophet Muhammad (ṣ), Joseph, David and Solomon.

Adam and Human Resolution

Adam was the first human to experience *khilafa*. One may ask: Why did God remove Adam from heaven? Did Adam commit a sin which subsequently entailed the punishment of all his descendants on earth? The answer to these questions clarifies the link between humans, this current life, and the afterlife. However, it is relevant to phrase these questions differently.

The Quran states that God informed the angels of His intention to place a vicegerent on earth. If the intention was to place Adam on earth to be the *khalifa*, then why was he

---

1. Ibid., p.28.

placed in heaven? The answer may be clarified as follows. Earth was the normal setting for Adam to fulfill his role as vicegerent and strive to adopt attributes of perfection and fulfill social harmony. It was important, though, for the first human to experience an exceptional introductory period for development[1] which qualified him to fulfill the demands of his role as vicegerent by understanding the difficulties of life and the conflict against Falsehood, and taking the correct decisions. This preparatory setting was a "garden":

> *"And: 'O Adam, dwell, you and your wife, in the Garden and eat from wherever you will but do not approach this tree, lest you be among the wrongdoers.'*
> (Quran 7:19)

Adam was provided with means of comfort in this "garden", but which are not available to all his descendants on earth:

> *"Indeed, it is for you that you will neither be hungery therein nor go naked.*
> *And indeed, you will not be thirsty therein nor be exposed to the heat of the sun."*
> (Quran 20:118-119)

With all of these conveniences, what is then required for development? The *khalifa* of God on earth is distinguished with various character traits, but the two most important qualities are knowledge and determination.

1-Knowledge is the light which illuminates your path. The first word of the Quranic revelation is *Irqa'*, meaning recite or read. God bestowed the highest knowledge upon Prophet Muhammad (ṣ), the greatest descendant of Adam, and God raises those who possess knowledge in ranks.

> *"Allah will raise those who have believed among you and those who were given knowledge, by degrees. And Allah is Acquainted with what you do."*
> (Quran 58:11)

---

1. Al-Sadr, Muhammad Baqer. Islam Leads Life, p.41.

As Jaluldin Rumi puts it:

"Knowledge is the Seal of the Kingdom of Solomon; the whole world is form, and knowledge is its spirit.

Because of this virtue, the creatures of the seas and those of hill and plain are helpless before man."[1]

2-Adam attained knowledge which would qualify him to become vicegerent on earth, but he still had not mastered self-restraint.

"And verily We commanded Adam, before, but he forgot; and We did not find in him determination."

(Quran 20:115)

Control of impulses enforces determination, leading you to overcome challenges and difficulties, conquer fear and anxiety, and attain your aims. The intellect produces sound judgment and aids in specifying perfection. Determination controls actions, conforming them to the intellect. Most of the sins which humans commit are a result of weak willpower. In contrast, your strengthened resolution prevents violation of divine law or the transgression of moral principles.

An individual enforces his willpower through experiences and confrontation of challenges. True remorse is constructive and serves in personal empowerment and resolve to change to the better. Once Adam ate of the tree and was evicted from the garden, he was spiritually shaken to the core and overcome by regret. He sensed his responsibility and his determination was strengthened in the ongoing confrontation with Satan, his sworn enemy who would spare no effort to lead him and his progeny astray. Such was the struggle of our forefather, the first *khalifa* on earth, which still endures with each and every one of us.

It is noteworthy that God describes the five greatest prophets -Muhammad (ṣ), Noah, Abraham, Moses and Jesus- as "those

---

1. Selected Poems of Rumi, p. 39.

of determination", specifically stating this quality despite the other commendable traits these noble prophets possessed.

> *"So be patient, [O Muḥammad], as were those of determination among the messengers."*
>
> (Quran 46:35)

God wants His servants to display firm determination. A tree which has sprung forth in the wild possesses a bark which is thick in density, standing firm in the face of violent winds and harsh weather conditions while domestically grown plants wilt and lose their vigor in unsuitable temperatures.[1] Likewise, humans need to enforce their willpower, bravely facing adverse conditions, refusing to yield to desires, and holding out against all temptations. Your actions reveal the level of your willpower; you can choose between two paths, displaying your inner strength by purifying your soul or succumbing to weakness and leading your spirit to perdition.

Upon considering Quranic verses and certain hadiths which seemingly cast the worldly life in a negative light, some might suppose that the world is an abominable place. A closer inspection of these texts, however, reveals that the worldly life in itself is not reviled, but the pursuit of the earthly life while disregarding the hereafter and refraining from seeking perfection is a cause for censure. Your existence on earth is a blessing because your conduct therein determines eternal bliss, so how could a blessing be disparaged? The following holy verse guides us to the importance of asking God for good in both this life *and* the hereafter:

> *"And among them is he who says, 'Our Lord, give us in this world [that which is] good and in the Hereafter [that which is] good and protect us from the torment of the Fire.'"*
>
> (Quran 2:201)

It is transmitted that this was the most often repeated supplication of Prophet Muhammad (ṣ). "This supplication is also frequently repeated by Muslims in their individual prayers

---

1. Refer to Imam Ali's letter to Othman bin Hanif..

and appears often in books of prayer. Good in this verse renders *hasanah*, which like many other words derived from the root h-s-n, has the sense of 'that which is beautiful'."[1]

Another verse clarifies how those who do good on earth shall be granted good, but reminds the believers that the hereafter is the lasting abode.

"For those who do good in this world is good; and the home of the Hereafter is better. And how excellent is the home of the pious."

(Quran 16:30)

Just as the "garden" was a preparatory and instructional setting for Adam to qualify to become a *khalifa*, the earthly life serves as a setting where human beings prepare for the eternal life. A baby spends nine months in its mother's womb, during which its organs develop and take shape in preparation for a life outside the womb. Likewise, our life on earth is transitory and preparatory for the afterlife, marked by exertion, difficulty and hardship.

"O man, indeed you are laboring toward your Lord laboriously [and] shall meet Him."

(Quran 84:6)

"We have certainly created man into hardship."

(Quran 90:4)

Man is expected to be in a constant state of fruitful activity. Earth is not a place for rest nor leisure, and one must exert a continuous effort and labor hard. Concentrate on the worship of your Lord and everything which makes you draw near to Him.

---

1. The Study Quran, p.208.

"For indeed with hardship there is ease, Indeed, with hardship there is ease. So when you have finished, toil. [1] And to your Lord direct [your] longing."

(Quran 94:5-8)

Have you noticed how you think you will be overjoyed when you reach a certain milestone, but only find yourself longing for more? You look forward to earning an academic degree, finding a job, marrying your soulmate, raising children, and fulfilling financial stability, but once you attain what you yearned for you notice that you have not attained complete satisfaction. Rumi states that:

"Within a human being is such a love, a passion and longing... a desire, that, even if he were to possess a hundred thousand worlds, he would still not find rest or peace. People try their hand at all sorts of trades and professions -they learn astronomy and medicine, and so forth- but they are not at peace because they haven't found what they are seeking. The beloved is called *dilaram* because the heart finds tranquility through the beloved, so how can it find tranquility through anything else? All these pleasures and objects of search are like a ladder. Ladder rungs are not places to stay and abide, but rather are to pass through. The sooner one awakens and becomes aware and watchful, the shorter the road becomes and the less one's life is wasted on these 'ladder rungs.'" [2]

The earth is not a place for rest, but a constant struggle toward perfection. Neither will material possessions grant you comfort, nor will fame or social status grant you serenity. The joy you feel upon attaining earthly riches is fleeting. Tranquillity lies only in the connection with God, He who

---

1. There are various translations for this verse, such as: "So when you are free, exert thyself".
Some interpretations are as follows: After completing the obligatory devotions, one should supplicate the Lord and perform supererogatory devotions, or when free from worldly affairs, one should pray. Or one should never cease to strive in the way of God nor cease to exert oneself more to do God's Will. It can also be taken to mean: When you are free from striving against your enemies, exert yourself in worshipping the Lord. The Study Quran, p.2787.
2. The Rumi Daybook, p.70.

loves you, shows you tenderness far greater than any mother's compassion, and aids you in all stages of your life. No matter the pain, the burden, the suffering, know that you will be granted solace and an everlasting reward.

"And be patient, for indeed, Allah does not waste the reward of those who do good."

(Quran 11:115)

"So no soul knows what has been hidden for them of comfort for eyes as a reward for what they used to do."

(Quran 32:17)

Remembrance of God not only has a calming and soothing effect, but also transforms the heart, imbuing it with light. "In the language of spiritual alchemy, the remembrance of God is described as an elixir that eventually turns the lead or base metal of the soul into pure gold. This is similar to when God's Majesty descends upon the heart through the act of remembrance: it acts as an elixir for the heart, gradually transforming it from a dark, murky substance into one that is pure, luminous, unchangeable, and able to 'see'. The heart is thus changed from its fallen state, symbolized by lead, to its state of perfection, symbolized by gold."[1]

"Those who have believed and whose hearts are assured by the remembrance of Allah. Verily, by the remembrance of Allah are hearts assured."

(Quran 13:28)

---

1 Ibid., p.1136.

*Praise be to God,
the Lord of the Worlds*

www.ingramcontent.com/pod-product-compliance
Lightning Source LLC
Chambersburg PA
CBHW051548010526
44118CB00022B/2627